THE IMAGE OF
THE INVISIBLE GOD

The
IMAGE
of the
INVISIBLE
GOD

ANTHONY TYRRELL HANSON

SCM PRESS LTD

334 00674 0

First published 1982
by SCM Press Ltd
58 Bloomsbury Street, London WC1

Typeset by Gloucester Typesetting Services
and printed in Great Britain by
The Camelot Press Ltd
Southampton

Contents

I wish to express my deep gratitude to my wife who has given me invaluable help with reading the proofs and compiling the indexes. I would also like to acknowledge my debt to John Bowden for his consideration and assistance in preparing the final draft of this work.

A.T.H.

One

The Contemporary Debate

Anyone who studies the history of the Christian church encounters from time to time periods of intense intellectual debate and conflict. The period from about AD 320 to AD 451 was one such epoch. Another occurred in Western Europe during the twelfth and thirteenth centuries, caused by the impact of the rediscovery of Aristotle. Of course the period of the Reformation was a third. We are certainly experiencing another time of debate and conflict in the Western church today.

The causes for this intellectual ferment go far back and are by no means simple or easily understood. The movement began in the seventeenth century, gathered momentum with the high Enlightenment of the eighteenth century, and took on new aspects with the scientific revolution in the nineteenth century. Were we to try to give a full account of it, we would have to mention the discoveries of science about the origin of the universe, of the world, and of man. We would have to explain what is meant by the modern understanding of historical research. Above all, we would be obliged to mention the emergence of biblical criticism as a technique common to all educated students of the Bible.

This book is concerned with only one aspect of Christian doctrine, the doctrine of the person of Jesus Christ, so we must be content with detailing what has been the impact of this contemporary movement of thought on that doctrine. It has meant, in effect, that one important element in the doctrine as traditionally expressed has been called into question, the element which is called in technical language 'the hypo-static union'. This means the claim that in the historical figure Jesus

Christ we encounter, not the person or personality of any human being at all, but the very person of the second member of the Trinity, the Son or Word of God. The term 'hypostatic' indicates that in Jesus Christ there was only one *hypostasis*, which is the nearest the ancients got to our modern concept of 'person'. It was held according to the traditional doctrine that this *hypostasis* or divine person was united to the humanity of Jesus. The mode by which it was united was never officially defined by the church, since this was exactly the point on which the two influential theological schools of Alexandria and Antioch disagreed. But all who accepted the famous Chalcedonian Formula acknowledged that there was only one *hypostasis* or individual personality in Jesus Christ, and that was the divine personality of the Word or Son of God.

The doctrine thus expressed owed a great deal to the picture of Jesus presented in the Fourth Gospel. If we only had the first three gospels, it is very doubtful indeed whether we would be inclined to think of Jesus as presenting a divine personality. The synoptic writers, though they all describe him as the Son of God, do not seem to see any incongruity in also describing him as exhibiting many of the characteristics of a human personality. He prays, he appears to be limited in knowledge at certain points, he even shows fear of death. Above all, he gives no hint that he knows anything of a pre-incarnate state. But when we turn to the Fourth Gospel we get a very different impression: there Jesus does not seem to be ignorant of anything; he openly declares his messiahship (rather a secret in the other gospels); he hints that he is 'equal with God'; he confesses his one-ness with the Father. He has awareness of a pre-incarnate existence ('before Abraham was I am'). He seems to possess a knowledge which he has brought from heaven. The author of the Fourth Gospel tells us in so many words that in him the eternal divine Logos or Word of God took flesh. There can be little doubt that the doctrine of the 'hypostatic union' was directly inspired by the Fourth Gospel.

But the great majority of competent scholars today have the gravest doubts about the historical accuracy of the picture of Jesus which we meet in the Fourth Gospel. The position is not, as it was among some radical critics of the last century, that the whole gospel is regarded as a work of sheer fiction. On the contrary, some elements in the Fourth Gospel are based on genuine historical tradition and can tell us something about the life of Jesus. But it is precisely those elements on which the doctrine of the hypostatic union is based that are historically most suspect. In other words, the picture of a Jesus who was essentially a divine rather than a human personality is probably a construction by the author of the Fourth Gospel. If we are to base our doctrine of the person of Jesus Christ on history rather than on a theological construction, we must begin from a Jesus who, whatever else he was, was unambiguously a human personality.

This has been well known to serious students of the Fourth Gospel for at least fifty years, but it is only just beginning to affect deeply the work of Christian theologians. Perhaps this is because there has been an increasing tendency towards specialization in theology as well as in every other discipline, and scholars of the New Testament have been content to get on with their work without concerning themselves with its consequences for theology. But such an attitude is hardly a responsible one. Most scholars of the New Testament are believing Christians, and they must have some regard to how their researches affect their belief. There is a certain obligation for a Christian scholar to interpret his conclusions and make them intelligible to educated Christians. The responsible expert on the New Testament must also be something of a theologian.

What is needed is a re-presentation of the doctrine of the person of Christ in such a way that the doctrine will not be based on the assumption that the Jesus of history is accurately pictured in the Jesus of the Fourth Gospel. But the traditional doctrine of the person of Christ, largely based (as we have seen) on the Fourth Gospel, was officially defined by the Council of Chalcedon in AD 451. Jesus Christ had one *hypostasis* or personal being, to which belonged two natures, an eternal divine nature which had always been that of the Word, and a human nature which the Word assumed at the time of the incarnation. In our search for an alternative to this doctrine we must therefore go behind Chalcedon. We must go back, to the extent that we can, behind even the Fourth Gospel, though this does not mean that we must repudiate the very valuable theological insights of that gospel. We shall find that in fact the New Testament, if properly understood, can help us in our quest. As Hans Küng has well remarked, the New Testament is much richer in christological material than the Chalcedonian theology alone would suggest.

3

Moreover, we can appeal to an analogous movement in the field of liturgy. What is called 'the liturgical movement' is now affecting every tradition in the Western church. This movement means in effect that the church, as far as its eucharistic practice is concerned at least, is going back to a pre-Constantinian pattern of worship. Over a very large area of the Western church today the form and practice of eucharistic worship finds its closest parallel in the worship of the church in the third and fourth centuries. This is, though many lay people are quite unaware of it, a vast reorientation in worship, quite as drastic as anything that was carried out by the Reformers of the sixteenth century. But the faithful on the whole seem to be accepting it, and within a generation it will come to be regarded as normal practice. Indeed, we might well claim that in our study of the doctrine of the person of Christ we are better off than are the liturgical experts, who, in every denomination, have drawn up new services, all sharing in a remarkable way the same pattern. They have very little positive evidence to work on before the end of the second century. For christological source material we have the New Testament itself.

I said above that this book was concerned with the doctrine of the person of Christ. But even that is an inaccurate statement: this book is in fact about the doctrine of the risen Christ, the mode of Christ's presence in the contemporary church. It forms a sequel to one I have already written on the doctrine of the incarnation as such. But in order that we may be able to tackle this question at the best point of departure, we must first briefly review recent work on the doctrine of the incarnation. In the course of that review the precise approach to the doctrine which I advocated in my first work will be outlined. Then we will be able to begin to determine what are the implications as far as concerns the question of the mode of Christ's presence in the church.

It would not be true to say that no theologians have reacted to the question mark which modern scholarship has put against the Chalcedonian christology. In fact a number of very eminent theologians have taken up the challenge either to vindicate Chalcedon against its critics, or to produce a satisfactory alternative christology. For the purpose of this review, I shall divide such theologians into four groups, all moderns in the sense that they have all written since the last World War.

4

1. The Anti-metaphysical school

I wish I could find a better name to characterize this group. But at least it indicates one leading characteristic they all share. They are all resolutely opposed to any attempt to link a doctrine of the person of Christ to any metaphysical scheme or even concept. In this sense no doubt they are all more or less influenced by the tradition of Karl Barth, though Karl Barth would undoubtedly have repudiated the theology of every one of them. I will mention three, Moltmann, Sobrino, and Käsemann. Most of their work on christology was written before 1975, but has only appeared in English since then. J. Moltmann in his book *The Crucified God*[1] rejects metaphysics in constructing a christology. He sees the crucifixion as the point *par excellence* where God is at work and claims that only a doctrine of God as Trinity does justice to the New Testament concept of the crucified God. He rejects the two-natures theory and strongly emphasizes God as the God of the future. His book has perhaps more to teach us about the doctrine of the atonement than about the incarnation. It is full of rhetoric and never clearly states how Jesus is God and man. In any case to attempt to dispense altogether with metaphysics in outlining a doctrine of the incarnation is in my opinion disastrous. Moltmann's christology is in some respects worked out more fully by J. Sobrino, in his book *Christology at the Crossroads*.[2] Sobrino represents Jesus as leading a movement against social oppression. Sobrino, like Moltmann, rejects metaphysics altogether; he sees Jesus as presenting in his life not God but the way to God. God is not an end in himself and is to be found in the oppressed and only there. This results in an ultra-Barthian rejection of all other ways of knowing God. Like Moltmann Sobrino obscurely retains a Trinitarian doctrine of God, though God is defined as a process in history as well as an ultimate mystery. He claims that one can only know God by means of *praxis* in following Jesus, not conceptually or through direct religious experience. This emphasis on *praxis* is derived directly from Marxism and is really a piece of outdated Marxist epistemology. Marx held that material objects impinging upon our brains produce true copies of themselves, which are our sensations. We verify whether these copies are true or not by practice. But practice only produces more sensations which come from images themselves in need of verification. In fact *praxis*, though certainly essential for those who wish to live the Christian life, cannot be used as a criterion for how we know God.

When we turn to Käsemann's christology we labour under the disadvantage that Käsemann has never written a book on christology as Moltmann has. His views have to be collected from a great variety of books and articles. I have therefore made extensive use of an immense book by P. Gisel, *Verité et Histoire*,[3] which reviews the whole of Käsemann's theology in a volume of nearly seven hundred pages. There are two fundamental elements in Käsemann's theology: God for him is revealed in history, but history is not therefore regarded as providing a pattern of events, or even as capable of revealing the absolute: God is revealed as particular in the relative and particular. And secondly he rejects any metaphysic of God, or of the knowing subject, or of faith.[4] Käsemann is so determinedly relativistic that he will not even speak of an absolute origin for Christianity. As far as concerns christology, Käsemann prefers a theology of the cross and of Luther's concept of God as *deus absconditus*, the God who conceals himself in the humility and horror of the cross. Jesus is not for Käsemann a being of two worlds, two substances, or two natures. He rejects the concept of God incarnate since this represents too reliable a scheme of things. It does not reflect the insecurity of the cross. It is also too manifest, it does not allow for a *deus absconditus*. Gisel writes: 'La verité de Dieu se dit dans la christologie.'[5] Käsemann defines faith as obedience, and this leads directly to a distinctly Marxist doctrine of God known in *praxis*. The test of the theology of the cross is action: you understand it by living it.[6] And consider this epigram of Gisel's 'Jésus est Dieu tout en n'étant pas Dieu'.[7] This might well be worked into a profound christology, but it cannot be said that Käsemann does that. Gisel also remarks that for Käsemann 'the Cross thus marks the end of all natural theology'.[8] It is not surprising therefore that we find in Käsemann a doctrine of God that has markedly fideist characteristics. Käsemann takes issue with Greek thought; with Aristotle as well as Plato. This was based, says Käsemann, on the mistaken assumption that the world as it is and truth are basically homogeneous. In fact thought is not adequate to represent reality. It follows therefore that the God of the Christian gospel is not necessary in the sense in which the word was understood in the Enlightenment. God is tied to contingence, because apparently there is nothing else. God is also a moving God; he does not merely cherish the world, he changes it. So truth comes through praxis. God must not be described as that which supports the world. In that case he could not be identified with Jesus crucified. He is received as promise and is to be found in the realm of the possible. God is not so much he who is, but rather he who cares.[9] With this Käsemann also maintains a doctrine of God as being in some sense Trinity: 'Christianity is partly tied to history, and that is why it thinks of the God whom it proclaims as in a Trinitarian mode.' The cross is the moment when God comes to himself. Hence the need for movement and for a doctrine of the Trinity.[10]

We seem to see in Käsemann's christology flashes of deep insight obscured by deep clouds of smoke. At times he seems almost perverse, especially in his insistence that God is only known in the particular and cannot be associated with any universal at all. God cannot be only particular. Käsemann's rejection of metaphysics, theism,[11] and natural knowledge of God constitutes in fact a form of fideistic irrationalism over which hovers the tormented shade of Nietzsche. A combination of Lutheran fideism and Marxist pragmatism, informed by the fiery personality of Ernst Käsemann produces a christology which is exciting and radical, but which answers none of the questions which I want to ask.

This is an appropriate point at which to discuss another significant work on Christian doctrine, Professor Maurice Wiles' book *The Remaking of Christian Doctrine*.[12] There is much in it that seems to me to be excellent sense. For example Wiles writes as follows about the Fourth Gospel: 'If the Fourth Gospel is understood to be a precise record of the *ipsissima verba* of Jesus, its significance as evidence for Christianity is vastly different from what it is if the Gospel is understood in any of the ways in which most modern scholars would regard it.'[13] This has by no means been fully accepted by all modern theologians. Karl Barth, for example, despite his paying lip service to biblical criticism, tends, in practice, to treat the Fourth Gospel as a reliable record in matters christological. And when we come below to consider Brian Hebblethwaite's work this is an issue which will prove important. But Wiles' main difficulty with any doctrine of the incarnation is that he does not like to ascribe absolute authority to any one particular occasion or set of circumstances in the world.[14] This would of course constitute just as great an objection to any doctrine of the incarnation as to the traditional one. But I cannot see that it is a very solid argument. Any doctrine of special revelation requires that certain events should be specially revelatory. I would have thought that Wiles' real difficulty must be with the Judaeo-Christian doctrine of God rather than with the doctrine of the incarnation, since both Jews and Christians have always held that God can and does act in certain historical situations. Wiles' objection would, in principle, be just as valid against the view that God had sent Israel into exile in Babylon and called them back.

A second difficulty which Wiles finds in the traditional doctrine of the incarnation concerns the question of evidence. He does not think that there is sufficient evidence to support the traditional doctrine: 'The information the theologian has traditionally looked for is simply not the kind of information that can properly be expected to be drawn from the evidence at our disposal by historical means.'[15] And later he asks whether the evidence requires an account of Jesus such as traditional orthodoxy gives, and concludes that it does not.[16] There is a sense in which I agree with Wiles here. Some theologians, notably Karl Barth, speak as if the conclusion that Jesus personally was God was an original datum of the experience of the first disciples and not a later construction. If the much abused book, *The Myth of God Incarnate*, has done nothing else but show that the Christian doctrine of the incarnation is a construction and not a datum of experience it will not have been written in vain, for all the vagaries of its various authors. But then any doctrine of the incarnation must be a construction. The real question is: what sort of construction did the original experience require? Wiles appears to conclude that it did not require any particular construction. This seems to me to be a purely arbitrary conclusion.

Finally, we should note another passage where he writes: 'Speaking of Jesus as the Son of God had a very different connotation in the first century from that which it has had ever since Nicaea. Talk of his pre-existence ought probably in most, perhaps in all, cases to be understood on the analogy of the Torah, to indicate the eternal divine purpose being achieved through him, rather than pre-existence of a fully personal kind.'[17] The first of these two sentences seems to me very true, though it must be observed that by the time the Fourth Gospel came to be written the title 'Son' as applied to Jesus had acquired very lofty associations indeed. But the second sentence (concerning pre-existence) is, I believe, completely astray. Indeed I cite very strong evidence to show that one can hold that Paul, the author of Hebrews, and John all believed in the existence of a pre-existent divine being distinguishable from God the Father, who manifested himself in the historical Jesus Christ. However I shall be discussing these points very fully in subsequent chapters, and I shall even at one place use the analogy of the Torah in a christological context.

2. *Roman Catholic Interpreters of Chalcedon*

Next, I wish to deal with a group of three Roman Catholic theologians all of whom may be regarded as interpreters of Chalcedon, in the sense that, though they wish to retain Chalcedon as the normative way of expressing the truth of the incarnation, they are fully aware of its difficulties for us today, and are anxious to find some way of expressing in terms intelligible to moderns the truth which Chalcedon was designed to defend.

In 1976 there was published an English translation of a book originally published in German by W. Kasper, a professor in the Catholic Faculty of Theology of Tübingen.[18] It is a very able discussion of the modern problem of expressing the meaning of the traditional doctrine of the incarnation. Kasper does not avoid any of the problems and is well acquainted with up to date criticism of the New Testament. Like Karl Rahner[19] he defends the Chalcedonian Formula, but he realizes that it needs to be expressed in modern terms. This is the passage in which he says most clearly what the doctrine of hypostatic union really means: 'Only within the idea of hegemony of the Logos is the possibility of a unity in distinction "intelligible", for only God can be thought of as so "supra-essential" and "surpassingly free" that he can posit in himself with its own identity what is distinct from him, precisely by uniting it wholly with himself.' Kasper is, of course, wrestling with the problem of reconciling the existence in Jesus of a complete human personality with the assertion that the person behind the outward appearance of Jesus of Nazareth was the eternal Word. I conclude from this very complicated formula of Kasper's that all he is saying in effect is that the hypostatic union is a mystery which we cannot understand, but all things are possible with God. I came to exactly the same conclusion in my own book *Grace and Truth* when I considered Karl Rahner's attempt to do what Kasper tries to do here.[20] If, however, the doctrine of the incarnation is an interpretation, as it must be, I do not see the advantage in offering an interpretation (in this case the doctrine of hypostatic union) which must in the last analysis be classified as a mystery. An interpretation is intended to explain. If total mystery is to be the conclusion, better say at the beginning that the co-existence in Jesus of divinity and humanity is an inexplicable mystery instead of espousing an explanation that must itself be explained in such obscure terms.

In my critique of Karl Rahner's account of the doctrine of the incarnation, already referred to in *Grace and Truth*, I noted how far he was willing to go in the acknowledgment of the existence of an independent human personality in Jesus, so much so that at times his language reminds one of Schleiermacher's. Now in his more recent work *Foundations of the Christian Faith*[21] he has clarified his position and seems to me to have moved so close to that adopted by D. M. Baillie, W. N. Pittenger and myself that I doubt if there is any substantial difference between us. It is true that he uses freely the phrases 'God-man' and 'hypostatic union' to describe the nature of the union of divinity and humanity in Jesus, but he does not seem to use these phrases in the sense in which they were intended by the Fathers of the fourth century AD. He writes: 'In Jesus, God's communication to man in grace, and at the same time its categorical self-interpretation in the corporeal, tangible and social dimension, have reached their climax, have become revelation in an absolute sense'.[22] He adds later: '(God) cannot simply be God himself as acting in the world, but must be a part of the cosmos'[23] and Rahner specifically denies that God disguised himself as man. The Logos, he continues, 'establishes (the material being of Jesus) as what is different from himself in such a way that this very materiality expresses *him*, the Logos himself, and allows him to be present in the world'.[24] A little later on he asks: 'Is the hypostatic union an absolutely higher level on which the bestowal of grace on a spiritual creature is surpassed, or is it a singular and unique moment in the universal bestowal of grace, which bestowal cannot even be conceived of without the hypostatic union of an individual person?'[25] Rahner opts for the second alternative. I may be misunderstanding Rahner here, but it seems to me that he would not accept J. H. Newman's famous verse:

And that a higher gift than grace
Should flesh and blood refine,
God's presence and his very self
And essence all divine.

In Jesus, according to Rahner, what we have is not 'a higher gift than grace', even though he calls it 'hypostatic union'.

However, Rahner says later that a merely moral union is not sufficient. It must be 'a union which eliminates the possibility of separation between the proclamation and the proclaimer'.[26] He defines the Logos as the possibility in God of his communicating with us in this way, and asserts that in Jesus 'the Word has assumed an individual human nature'.[27] Then he goes on to write: 'The incarnation of God is the unique and highest instance of the actualization of the essence of human reality'.[28] He claims that this is an ontological union: 'The true being of spirit is itself spirit', and rejects the notion that 'God has set things right on earth in the livery of a human nature which is joined to Him only extrinsically'. He meets the objection to this account of Jesus, that what he says of Jesus could in principle be true of any man who was completely open to God's grace. Rahner answers the objection in essentially the same way that D. M. Baillie does (see below), though he uses different terms: 'historicity and personhood must not be reduced to the level of nature'; i.e. grace is supernatural and is the gift of the electing God.[29]

When he turns to an explanation of how the divinity and humanity in the incarnate Word operated, he appears to come even closer to the position maintained in *Grace and Truth*: 'This precise humanity (i.e. Jesus of Nazareth) is then the self-expression of God'.[30] Later he adds that Jesus had a human self-consciousness which operated normally, though he does refer obscurely to 'an unreflexive consciousness in the depths of his being' as well.[31] Rahner does not develop this thought. Perhaps it could be a means of maintaining a 'two-nature' doctrine on Chalcedonian lines. But later he writes that the humanity is too easily thought of as a livery and adds that when we say the historical Jesus was God we mean it in a different sense from that which we mean when we say that Peter was a man.[32] Rahner denies that there was a single centre (of personality? of consciousness?), a divine one. Jesus existed as 'a created centre of activity vis-à-vis God'. He makes free decision, 'he has new experiences that surprise him'.[33] Finally, he suggests that if you push the concept of Jesus as the man given over to God far enough you reach what he calls an 'ontic Christology'.[34]

We may surely conclude from this that Karl Rahner, having quite justifiably abandoned the ancient concepts of 'substance' and 'nature' as applied to the incarnate Word, is in fact left with an understanding of the relation of the divine Word to Jesus which does not differ essentially from that which we find in D. M. Baillie, in Pittenger, and in my own book. He is able to apply terms such as 'ontological', 'hypostatic union' and 'ontic' to this relationship because of the element of existentialism in his philosophic background, but he does not mean that Jesus was ontologically God in the way in which the Fathers of Chalcedon meant it. Indeed I would conjecture that only his remarkable skill in using traditional language in an untraditional sense has prevented him from being summoned before the same array of inquisitors that has already confronted the unfortunate Edward Schillebeeckx. For all intents and purposes Karl Rahner may be said to present a doctrine of the mode of the incarnation that goes as far as the most extreme version of Nestorianism known to the ancients. I think he is to be applauded for this, but in the interests of clarity I think it ought to be acknowledged.

It may well seem premature to discuss the christology of Schillebeeckx at this moment in time: only two volumes of what is planned as a three volume work have been published in English. Schillebeeckx himself has been undergoing examination at the hands of the authorities in his own church to decide whether his approach is sufficiently in accord with traditional orthodoxy. Indeed his case may well be a test as to whether scholars in Roman Catholic orders are to be permitted to engage in free christological debate or not. Moreover, Schillebeeckx himself tells us that his main christological contribution is to be made in volume three. Nevertheless, he is a theologian of no mean quality. His first volume has been very widely read and discussed. It would seem strange to undertake a review of significant christological work since 1975 and to leave him out. I therefore include a consideration of his first and second volumes.[35]

His first volume is principally an examination of what biblical criticism and historical research can tell us about the historical Jesus. But inevitably it has christological implications and these become more frequent towards the end of the book. Schillebeeckx has some very well justified preliminary comments: 'The divine in (Jesus) is not something given apodeictically.'[36] Again, 'the Christian Trinitarian interpretation of the living God is the result or implication of a refusal on the part of Christians to identify Jesus absolutely, without distinctions, with the living God'.[37] He also remarks that 'from Nicaea onwards one particular christological model, the Johannine, has been developed as a norm within very narrow limits'.[38] These are all considerations which anyone with a scholarly understanding of the New Testament must accept as a starting point for a reflection on christology, but which are too often ignored by pure theologians, who tend sometimes to assume that what they call 'the divinity of Jesus' was an original datum of the experience of the first disciples.

Next, Schillebeeckx claims that when we consider the career of Jesus we can use two languages about the same event, one secular and one of faith. These correspond to the human and the divine in traditional parlance.[39] Schillebeeckx uses the term 'enhypostasia' for 'the being in, of, and through God which belongs to everyone'.[40] When speaking of Jesus we must not speak of two components, but rather of two aspects.[41] A little later on he becomes more specific: 'the Word of God is the undergirding ground of the whole Jesus phenomenon'.[42] 'Through and in the person of the man Jesus God is manifest to us as an interpersonal relationship between the Father, Jesus Christ, and the Holy Spirit'.[43] 'As a revelation of God, therefore, Jesus does not constitute that in God which corresponds to the "Son of God", the Father, and the Spirit. The man, Jesus is indeed the ground that enables us to denote the intra-trinitarian reality called in the context provided by the man Jesus, Son of God'.[44] Thus far Schillebeeckx would seem to be saying that Jesus is in fact a revelation of the divine Word or eternal Son, but is not personally identical with the Second Person of the Trinity, precisely the position I took in *Grace and Truth*.

Schillebeeckx does however seem to advance a step nearer the Chalcedonian definition, for he writes that Jesus 'within the limits of a human and personal mode of being', did 'live out the essential nature of a divine person, that is, to be himself in radical self-giving to the other'.[45] And on the next page he adds that the Word of God is the self-communication of the Father, and in this we see God. He therefore concludes that there was an hypostatic 'identification' (a word he prefers to 'union') between the Word and Jesus and that therefore Jesus cannot rightly be called 'a human person'. But he strongly repudiates the notion of anhypostasia, the view that the human nature of Jesus was without a personal centre. His final word in this book is: 'Through his historical self-giving, accepted by the Father, Jesus has shown us who God is: a *Deus humanissimus*'.[46]

Ironically enough, further light on Schillebeeckx's position is provided by the answer which he prepared for his inquisitors in December 1979. This is printed in Peter Hebblethwaite's book about the questioning of Schillebeeckx and Küng, *The New Inquisition?*[47] Among other points, Schillebeeckx had to explain what he meant by his use of the phrase 'Jesus as a human person'. He writes: 'I never speak of the human person of Jesus, but of Jesus who is "personally human" . . . I say that his way of being human is personalist, and nothing more. Only once do I use the expression "human person" in the ontological context but then it is precisely to *deny* that the Christ can be called a human person . . . In this way I wanted to safeguard the understanding of Chalcedon and at the same time a contemporary understanding.' This position is further clarified:

> I simply deny that there was anything lacking in the humanity of Jesus (just as St Thomas denies it). But I also know by experience that the idea that 'another' person can personalize in 'human nature' is incomprehensible for most of our readers. How then can one make sense of the dogma? I did this by means of the notion of *hypostatic identification*, i.e. not a union of two persons, human and divine, but an (of course ontological) identification of the second person of the Trinity with a formally spiritual human nature. In my opinion that is the traditional hypostatic union in its pure form.

Schillebeeckx's second volume, *Christ: the Christian Experience in the Modern World*, sheds very little further light on his christology. He writes: 'the nature of God's divinity has been revealed historically in Jesus' life . . . Resurrection is the continuation of the personal life of Jesus, as a man beyond death . . . God identifies himself with the person Jesus, just as Jesus identified himself with God.'[48] And of the resurrection of Jesus he writes: 'His living communication with man is thus restored in a very real way, difficult though it is to describe' – which gives us no clue as to how Schillebeeckx believes the risen Jesus is related to believers. A final quotation may be added though it does not seem to advance the argument: '*either* Jesus was just a man like all of us, in which case his claim rests on an illusion, *or* as man he was so at one with a completely different reality which we call God that this divine reality did not in any way compete with his humanity.'[49]

After reading this, I find it difficult to identify any real difference between Schillebeeckx's christology and that which I defended in *Grace and Truth*. He seems to me to be saying in effect that behind the human personality of Jesus we encounter the divine Word of God addressing us. This I would, of course, freely accept. I do not think that, any more than Karl Rahner, he would be willing to say 'God walked the roads of Galilee, etc.'. I do not think he would even commit himself to the crude statement 'Jesus *was* the Second Person of the Trinity'. I would certainly agree that in the historical Jesus we do encounter God addressing us as intimately and personally as is possible short of an apodeictic miracle or a purely private religious experience. But the analogy is Hosea or Jeremiah rather than Krishna or Dionysius. If either Karl Rahner or Edward Schillebeeckx chooses to call this relationship 'hypostatic union' or 'hypostatic identification' that is their affair. God forbid that I should give any encouragement to the misguided officials of the Roman Catholic Church who are harrying Schillebeeckx for his courageous attempts to make modern sense of ancient dogmatic formulae! But I cannot believe that either Rahner or he really means the same thing in their doctrine of the incarnation as did the Fathers of Chalcedon. Neither of these means by that doctrine a personal identity between the Word of God and Jesus, nor a natural union. But this is, I believe, what the Chalcedonian Formula implies. It may be that when we have access to Schillebeeckx's third volume we will be able to judge whether my conclusion is correct. In any case, a consideration of the main theme of this book, the relation of the risen Christ to the Word of God and to faithful Christians, must bring this issue out into the open.

3. A Modern Defender of Chalcedon

I now consider a modern theologian who defends rather than interprets the Chalcedonian Formula. He is Brian Hebblethwaite, Dean of Queens' College, Cambridge. I refer first to an essay which he wrote in 1972 as part of a symposium.[50] It consists mostly of general consideration about the doctrine of the incarnation. Thus, he writes: 'the purely human Christ, however open to the will of God, cannot possibly bear the weight of significance which is still attributed to him.'[51] In the phrase 'purely human' we have the problem pin-pointed. It is in the process of describing how he is divine that defenders of traditional christology often seem to lose the completeness of the humanity. A little later on he warns us that 'we cannot make our contemporary experience absolute'.[52] I for one would not want to do this. At most I am offering an alternative christology. Many defenders of the Chalcedonian Formula, including certainly Schillebeeckx's inquisitors, seem to want to make the fifth-century experience absolute. Hebblethwaite becomes more specific when he writes: 'it is of the essence of Christian theism that the eternal incomprehensible God is to be met and known in a particular man'.[53] This I would certainly accept. This essay seems to be in fact a defence of the use of the term 'substance' in christology, on the grounds that you cannot define everything in terms of events, because events happen to things. A purely functional christology must lead to an ontological christology. Once again, I can only agree. Indeed, I believe we can see this process taking place within the pages of the New Testament.

Brian Hebblethwaite becomes much more specific in an article entitled 'Incarnation – the Essence of Christianity?' which he wrote in 1977.[54] He refers to: 'the central belief of Christians that God himself without ceasing to be God, has come amongst us, not just in but *as* a particular man, at a particular time and place . . . The human life lived and the death died have been held quite literally to be the human life and death of God himself in one of the modes of his own eternal being'.[55] This use of the dangerous word 'literally' characterizes Hebblethwaite's account of the incarnation. He goes on to defend the traditional doctrine on the grounds that it insists on 'the direct personal encounter between God and man made possible by the Son of God's coming amongst us as one of us'.[56] My objection to the traditional doctrine is precisely that it does not do this: one who is not a human person is not really one of us. His second point is that only the traditional doctrine represents God as himself coming to grips with the power of evil, not just sending a representative.[57] This is an effective point, but I suspect that in fact the traditional doctrine only enables us to say this by means of the convention known as the *communicatio idiomatum*, whereby statements that really belong to one nature can by a *façon de parler* be applied to the other. When one asks, 'did the eternal Word of God actually die?' the orthodox answer has to be 'No. God cannot die. Only his human nature died.' Then Hebblethwaite indicates his own preference in explaining how this traditional christology can best be understood today. He opts for a 'kenotic' model.[58] This, he says, is 'a way of picturing the incarnation' but 'incarnation is not itself one of these models. Rather it is what is being pictured in these various inadequate ways'. Once again we have an emphasis on the literal meaning of the incarnation, as if incarnation itself was an original datum not a construction. He repeats 'the moral and religious force of Jesus' life and death depend on his *being* God incarnate', and describes his doctrine of the incarnation as 'one way of construing the self-revelation of God to man'.[59] Thus he would regard the fact of incarnation as a basic datum, but his model of a kenotic doctrine as a construction. At the very end of the article he does remark that the historical question is one which he has not examined and that much depends on it.

Hebblethwaite's third contribution is found in a collection of essays and comments published as a sequel to *The Myth of God Incarnate*.[60] Brian Hebblethwaite contributes various remarks. In an essay called 'The Incarnation and Modern Theology' he reaffirms his commitment to a doctrine of kenosis[61] and his belief that 'incarnation' is to be understood literally, like 'God' or 'sin'.[62] In a second essay, 'The Moral and Religious Value of the Incarnation', he criticizes the grounds on which John Hick rejects a kenotic approach, i.e. that it presents us with a 'paradox of God incarnate who does not know that he is God incarnate'. I would agree with Hebblethwaite here. Indeed I would go farther and say that if God incarnate knows that he is God incarnate he cannot really be God incarnate. But Hebblethwaite gets round the difficulty by an explicit theory of two distinct consciousnesses in the person of the eternal Word incarnate:

But in fact the tradition has carefully distinguished what can be said of the human subject, from what can be said of the divine subject, God the Son, whose human expression and vehicle in his incarnate life the human subject, Jesus, is. (As such, of course, it is uniquely not an independent human subject – hence the doctrine of 'anhypo-stasia'). Clearly, God, *qua* God, is aware of who he is and what he is doing, but *qua* man (i.e. as Jesus) his self-awareness is limited to a filial sense of dependence on the Father. For this reason incarnational christology attributes two consciousnesses, not to Jesus, but to God incarnate.[63]

It could not be put more clearly, though whether all the Fathers of Chalcedon would have been happy with this free use of the phrase 'two subjects' in the Word incarnate is doubtful. But Hebblethwaite has committed himself not only to a doctrine of two consciousnesses but also to a doctrine of 'anhypostasia', a word apparently never used by the ancients.[64] This is remarkably bold. Most defenders of Chalcedon today draw back from this.

Hebblethwaite has further clarified his position in an article pub-lished recently in the *Scottish Journal of Theology*[65] called 'The Propriety of the Doctrine of the Incarnation as a way of Interpreting Christ'. After a review of recent Anglican work on the doctrine of the incarna-tion, he quotes with approval Austin Farrer: 'He (Jesus) was not a copybook man-in-general, he was a Galilaean carpenter, a free-lance rabbi.' This certainly suggests a genuine human personality. He then proceeds to sketch a kenotic approach. The incarnation, he says, in-volved 'genuine growth, limited knowledge, and a restricted con-ceptual horizon'. He is willing to go even farther than this: 'It is highly implausible for us ... to suppose that Jesus knew himself to be or thought of himself as divine.' On the other hand Hebblethwaite is determined to preserve an ontological, metaphysical connection be-tween the historical Jesus and the eternal Son or Word: 'We cannot present kenotic Christology in such a way as to imply the abandonment of the divine functions of the Logos. ... The Blessed Trinity was per-fectly well aware of what was being done, experienced, and suffered. This is not to attribute two consciousnesses to Jesus. But it is to assert that the consciousness of the man Jesus was the limited human expres-sion of the omniscient divine consciousness.' He adds that Jesus' will was likewise the earthly expression of the divine will.

So far, I believe I could accept this description of the historical Jesus *toto corde*. But now Hebblethwaite brings in the metaphysical link which he considers so essential. He writes that in Jesus the divine nature took to itself 'the human nature of the man Jesus as a finite vehicle of God's very presence in our midst'. Even this I could accept, as long as the mode of the taking is described as *kat' eudokian* and not *kath' hupostasin* (by indwelling and not by ontological union). Hebblethwaite even adds (perplexingly as it seems to me): 'We cannot suppose that the divine Logos took the place of some element in the human being of Jesus.' But he adds 'the metaphysical subject of the human life of Jesus was the eternal Son of God'. But surely to say this is to assert that the divine Logos did take the place of some element in the human life of Jesus, and that the most central element of all, the human personality, what the Alexandrians would call the *hypostasis* and the Antiochenes the *prosōpon*. I confess I cannot see how Hebblethwaite can avoid this conclusion if he is to hold on to what he believes to be an essentially Chalcedonian account of the mode of the incarnation.

He does devote some space to the question of pre-existence. He writes: 'It is not the pre-existence of the humanity of the man Jesus' and he describes the risen Christ thus: 'The risen and ascended Christ is God the Son permanently expressed and focussed for us through the incarnate humanity', which seems to me to put the position very satisfactorily. It does not look as if Hebblethwaite would agree with the suggestion supported by Karl Barth and C. F. D. Moule that we must believe in a pre-existent person Jesus Christ.[66]

At the end of his article he briefly discusses the question of history, and here, as in the question of Jesus' self-consciousness, he makes considerable concessions. He writes: 'It is no longer possible to defend the divinity of Christ by reference to the claims of Jesus. . . . We may still wish to say that the divinity was manifest in the humanity; but this is not an impartial historical judgment. It is said only with hindsight in the light of the Resurrection and of the spiritual and sacramental experience of Christians ever since.' And almost his last words are to the effect that a purely historical reconstruction of the life of Jesus must at least be compatible with the interpretation which he defended. This is illuminating, since it implies that any doctrine of incarnation is an interpretation, not an original datum. What is still lacking, however, is the realization of the extent to which the interpretation Hebblethwaite advances is dependent on the Fourth Gospel's presentation of Jesus. He does not yet seem to have asked himself how far that presentation may be responsible for the account of Jesus which he defends, and how far therefore either account, St John's or his, may be reconciled with the evidence of the other three gospels.

4. *An Alternative Christology that does not dispense with Metaphysics*

Finally, we must consider three theologians who seem to come in an intermediate position between groups 1 and 2 as defined above. These all have in common a desire to elaborate a christology that avoids the difficulties of Chalcedon, but which also involves a Logos doctrine. They are distinguished from group 1 by the fact that, far from eschewing metaphysics, they all see the need of a link between a doctrine of the incarnation and at least some metaphysical concepts: and they differ from groups 2 and 3 because they do not make any attempt to base their christology on the Chalcedonian Formula. Moreover, they are more closely linked to each other than are the members of any of the other groups because in this group each later writer is consciously trying to build on the work of his predecessor. With considerable temerity I have included myself as the third member of this group, not because I would challenge comparison with those two other distinguished theologians, but because I did treat them as my inspiration, and it was from them that I began the account of the doctrine of the incarnation which I outlined in *Grace and Truth*. Since chapter two is an extension and sequel to that book, it is necessary that a resumé of *Grace and Truth* should come at the end of this chapter.

The first writer is D. M. Baillie, who in 1947 published his study of the incarnation *God was in Christ*. He begins from the assumption that, whatever else Jesus was, he was certainly a complete human personality. He advances from this to expound what he calls 'the paradox of grace'. Jesus was a man completely obedient to God, more so than any one else. But just because of this his life was a miracle of God's grace. Of course, he meets the objection: 'then you say that Jesus was just an ordinary man'. He answers that there is nothing ordinary about being completely obedient to God. Such a life can only have been lived by the grace of God; hence it was an act, or action of God. Jesus' life was supernatural, because it was a life fully endowed by God's grace; but it was not superhuman in the sense that Jesus disposed of powers or of knowledge not accessible to normal human nature. Baillie can therefore speak of God being incarnate in Jesus, the Son of God being manifest in Jesus, without accepting the Chalcedonian premiss that there was no centre of human personality in him.

W. N. Pittenger built on this foundation in his book *The Word Incarnate*.[67] He fully accepted Baillie's account of Jesus' human nature, but he criticized Baillie (with much justification) on the grounds that Baillie had never clearly indicated what was continuous between the eternal Son of God and Jesus. This deficiency he supplied by boldly adopting a Logos doctrine. It was, says Pittenger, the eternal Word, consubstantial with the Father, who dwelt in Jesus. But Pittenger defines the nature of that indwelling carefully. It was *kath' endokian*, he says, not *kath' hupostasin*; in other words, the nature of the link between the eternal Word and Jesus was the same as that which can be observed, though much less perfectly, in the lives of the saints. It was not some metaphysical, substantial link, such as *kath'hupostasin* requires. This is of course precisely the difference between the schools of Antioch and Alexandria in the ancient church. Pittenger adopted the Antiochene explanation. We should also say that Pittenger clearly states that in his account the divinity of the Son is manifested by means of the humanity of Jesus, though he does not work out the implications of this very fully.

It was on the basis of these two books that I elaborated my account of the doctrine of the incarnation in *Grace and Truth*. I began by taking the theme of 'grace and truth' or 'love and faithfulness' as the normative attributes of God in the great theophany in Exodus 34, and I traced this phrase through the Old Testament, showing how again and again it was associated with a definition or at least a description of God's nature. I claimed that this phrase, pointing to the theophany in Exodus 34, lies behind the expression of the incarnation of the Word in John 1.14 'full of grace and truth', and that John is claiming the Exodus theophany as having been in fact an appearance of the pre-existent Word. I found essentially the same theme in two passages in Romans, showing that Paul also saw Jesus as the revelation of God's nature as love. I next traced the theme in the synoptic gospels and other parts of the New Testament. Jesus was seen as the revelation of God's nature as love.

I then examined both the Fourth Gospel and Paul's acknowledged letters and found in them the assertion that God's nature was actually revealed in the complete manhood of Christ, in other words that the divinity was manifested in the humanity. This is closely related to the cross in both writers, so that, for those who have faith, the nature of God is seen most clearly at the point where Jesus was most completely devoid of superhuman characteristics. This led on to a presentation of the resurrection of Jesus as the great act whereby God vindicated both himself and his servant; and I drew a comparison with Jeremiah and the Servant of the Lord in Deutero-Isaiah. I followed with a chapter in which I tried to explain the genesis of the doctrine of the pre-existence of Christ in the New Testament, and suggested that if you hold, as I do, that the nature of God was revealed in the complete humanity of Jesus, you must be able to say how you recognize God. Apart from the question of the resurrection, with which I had already dealt, I claimed that we recognize God in Christ because we already know something of God from the revelation recorded in the Old Testament. I then acknowledged my debt to the approach to the doctrine of the incarnation outlined first by D. M. Baillie and then by W. N. Pittenger. Taking my cue from the account of the relation of God to Jesus expounded in Pittenger's work, I claimed that such a doctrine imperatively demanded a doctrine of God that sees him as Three-in-One, and went on to outline a doctrine of the Trinity based on the revelation of God's nature in Jesus Christ rather than on the revelation of an ontological link between God and Jesus.

This was, in historical terms, an ultra-Nestorian doctrine of the person of Jesus Christ. In a final chapter I compared it with the work of some other modern theologians such as Pannenberg and also those moderns who defend the traditional doctrine of hypostatic union. My approach depended very much on the concept of the final and normative revelation of God's very nature in the life, death and resurrection of Jesus Christ, and I insisted that this revelation could not be adequately comprehended or safeguarded without connecting it with the Word of God understood as a distinction within the Godhead. That was why I ended my exposition of the incarnation by reaffirming my belief in the doctrine of the Trinity. But my approach did assume that there was nothing 'superhuman' in Jesus Christ. Though he was God's chosen servant, elected to be the means of the supreme revelation of the Word, and thereby also the agent of God's unique act of redemption, he was not God in the sense in which the Chalcedonian Formula said he was. Jesus the unique revelation of God was not identified with the person of the divine Word.

Apart from the shock which this departure from traditional christology must cause to all orthodox Christians, it posed for me one problem which I hardly considered at all in *Grace and Truth*, the problem of the status, and the relation to believers of the risen and exalted Jesus Christ. I did in fact devote some two and a half pages to this question, but they are very sketchy and inadequate. This present work is an attempt to deal with this problem more adequately. I have not seen any reason since the publication of *Grace and Truth* to alter my fundamental approach to the doctrine of the incarnation. I still hold that we must begin by seeing Jesus 'from below', as Pannenberg puts it, and this means we must regard him as actually having been a complete human personality. I still hold that if you say Jesus was a complete human personality you cannot also hold the doctrine of hypostatic union (though I think there are many who hold both these beliefs in a confused way). I still believe that the only satisfactory model for the union of God and man in Jesus is that which we meet in actual experience, God's mode of indwelling in the saints, the doctrine which the Antiochene school of theology called indwelling *kat'eudokian*, 'according to God's good will'. I still believe that a doctrine of God as Trinity is essential in order to make sense of my account of the incarnation.

Two

The Traditional Doctrine of the Risen Christ

Since we have now reached the point where we can begin to examine the main question with which this work is concerned, we ought to state that question in unambiguous terms. In *Grace and Truth* I outlined a christology according to which Jesus was the unique, normative, and supreme revelation of God's character, peculiar instrument of the divine Word in his approach to men, but not ontologically united to God in a way impossible to the rest of mankind, and therefore not 'superhuman'. He was raised from the dead by God's power, an act of vindication which declared him to be the unique agent of God; he appeared to his disciples, and he entered into the eternal dimension which awaits all who are faithful to what they know of God. The question is this: how is this risen Christ related to the divine Word now, and how related to faithful Christians? Before attempting an answer, we would do well to see how traditional christology coped with this question.

The question of course was posed in somewhat different terms for traditional christology. In this tradition we have a single divine person, the eternal Word, or Son, who has assumed a complete human nature. The question then is: what happened to that human nature after the resurrection? As a matter of fact the question is rather more complicated than that, because traditional orthodoxy had to account, not just for a human nature, but for Jesus' body. So the question tended to take the form: what happened to the Lord's body after the ascension? Naturally this also involved asking how the risen Lord's humanity was related both to the eternal Word and to the faithful after the ascension. The heterogeneous and fragmentary nature of the accounts which the gospels give of the Lord's resurrection appearances allowed much scope for speculation about the nature of the risen body and there is no unanimity in the orthodox tradition as to the location of the Lord's body after the resurrection.

We should bear in mind as we review the Patristic tradition on this question how much the Platonic philosophical presuppositions of most of the Fathers influenced their thinking. The problem was to explain how the resurrection and glorification of Jesus' body could affect us: theologians who regard the universal idea as the ultimate reality, and physical particulars as lacking in ultimate reality, can do this more easily. They will either spiritualize the body, or fall back on an apophatic mysticism. In the examples which I give below we can see that Gregory of Nyssa in effect spiritualized the risen body of the Lord. But his Platonism could also help him by its generalizing tendency. Rivière, for instance, writes: 'Gregory's system may be sufficiently explained by the supernatural solidarity which he believes to exist between Christ, the head of mankind, and us who are its members; in this way the Saviour can easily be considered as the representative and type of mankind in general without its being necessary for him to have had in himself any concentrated essence of humanity.'[1] In similar vein H. E. W. Turner writes of the Eastern tradition: 'To this tradition physical and spiritual are not so much regarded as juxtaposed, as interpenetrating in a manner which the West simply has no terms to express.'[2] We shall find therefore that it is Western theologians who will experience the greater difficulty in making sense of the doctrine of the Lord's risen body.

On the question of the place of the risen body one can distinguish two schools of thought among the Fathers: the majority were content to say that when Jesus Christ ascended into heaven he took with him his risen body; thus Tertullian says that Jesus retains in heaven that same flesh which he assumed at the incarnation.[3] Hippolytus also believes that the Lord's flesh was taken up into heaven.[4] This implied the existence of a local heaven, but such a belief was by no means incompatible with ancient thought. There was also a tendency among the Fathers to distinguish the function of the glorified humanity from that of the Second Person of the Trinity. In his book *He Ascended into Heaven*, J. G. Davies quotes a sermon attributed to Chrysostom as saying that whenever God is disposed to punish men for their sins, 'seeing the sinless humanity at his right hand, he is placated'.[5] Another anonymous homilist, who may be Nestorius, claims that the 'one like unto a Son of man' of Daniel 7.13 refers not to the entire Word but to the risen humanity of Christ.[6] Obviously this sort of distinction was bound to bring problems when the relationship of the risen Christ to the faithful on earth came into consideration.

On the other hand there was another school of thought among the Fathers who, realizing the difficulties which emphasis on the reality and corporeality of the Lord's risen body would produce, tended to try to avoid them by presenting a spiritualizing account of the risen body. Not surprisingly, Origen is one of these. As Davies puts it: 'Convinced that God cannot be circumscribed locally and that the Son cannot therefore be deemed to move spatially when He is said to descend or ascend, he interpreted the Ascension in a manner not unacceptable in the twentieth century, as concerned with spiritual exaltation rather than with physical motion.'[7] Hilary also followed this line of thought. He wrote: 'For the nature of the earthly body does not secure this ascension except by being transformed into celestial glory.'[8] Thus Hilary interprets I Cor. 15.28 to mean that at the eschaton the subjection of the Son to the Father implies 'the absorption of the human by the divine, the transfiguration of the human in such wise that no trace of the earthly body will remain.'[9] A. J. Tait concludes that 'Hilary appears to have regarded Our Lord's human nature as dispensational only'.[10] Cassian also espoused this view. He writes: 'We no longer know Christ according to the flesh, because when bodily infirmity has been absorbed by divine majesty, nothing remains in that sacred body from which weakness of the flesh can be known in it. And thus whatever formerly belonged to a two-fold substance has become attached to a single power since there is no sort of doubt that Christ, who was crucified through human weakness, lives entirely through the glory of his divinity.'[11] We can find the same tendency in Athanasius: in *Orationes contra Arianos* III, 48 he argues that while he was in the flesh the Son was ignorant in his manhood, but omniscient in his divinity, and hence he explains Mark 13.32. But after his resurrection, when questioned about the future by the disciples in Acts 1, he does not confess ignorance. This was because his humanity had been divinized: 'Our Lord's human nature had now risen from the dead, and had put off its mortality and had been deified (*theopoiētheisa*)'. This spiritualizing school, though it did not prevail in Western tradition, is very significant, since it suggests that from certain points of view the humanity of the risen Lord was an embarrassment to Christian theologians.

One of the best examples of this school is Marcellus of Ancyra; he is significant because, though he was ultimately condemned for heresy, he certainly influenced Gregory of Nyssa, who is regarded by Eastern Christians as the very flower of orthodoxy. Nearly all we know of Marcellus' teaching is to be found in the book which Eusebius of Caesarea wrote against his teachings. But Eusebius gives very extensive quotations. Marcellus rejected the usual concept of the relation of the Logos to God, that the Logos was a distinguishable *hypostasis* or individual entity. This puts him at the opposite pole from Arius, who was only too ready to distinguish the Logos, since he regarded him as a creature in the last analysis. But Marcellus' position made him very sensitive to anything that might seem to separate the Logos from the Father, and of course the humanity of the Word falls into this category. He could not deny that the Word had taken flesh, but he wished to be rid of the association as soon as possible. He therefore so interpreted I Cor. 15.28 as to mean that after the parousia the Logos would be divested of the manhood. Eusebius expresses Marcellus' theory thus: 'that flesh which he (the Logos) assumed is to be left on its own, and the Word which had pre-existed in God is to be separated from his body (even though that body is immortal and incorruptible), and merged with God, so that God will resume the same state as he originally possessed.'[12] Marcellus certainly did set himself a problem, since he seemed to be leaving the flesh very much on its own. Thus he claims that when Jesus said 'I and the Father are one', he only referred to the Logos part of him, which was identical with the Father. He did not refer to the flesh, which could in fact speak about its own will: 'Not my will, but thine, be done' (II,2,23–24 (38–9)). A great principle with Marcellus, which we shall find reproduced in Gregory of Nyssa, is that the ultimate state of things must be identical with the original state. But originally of course there was no flesh associated with the godhead. Marcellus writes: 'Before the creation of the world, nothing existed except God alone'; at the end of the world therefore the Word will return to the Father's being and all will be as it was before the creation (II,2,28 (39); 39–40 (41)). He protests a little later that the flesh, which profits nothing, and is the form of a slave, can hardly be a permanent consort to the Word, who is to exist through the ages to come (II,3,5–7 (44)). It is interesting to note that Marcellus also rejected the notion, which we shall find in Augustine and in some modern theologians, that in some sense the manhood of the Son pre-existed before the incarnation. He makes much of the phrase 'image of the invisible God', saying that the image of the invisible must itself be visible, and that these words must therefore only apply to the incarnate Christ, not to any pre-existent being (I,3,26–27 (47)). This should logically imply that the phrase is no more applicable after the ascension, when the Word was no longer visible; but in fact Marcellus holds that the Word retains his flesh until after the parousia, and only then gets rid of it (II,3,5 (51)).

In one passage Marcellus seems to suggest that the flesh had a limiting effect on the Word during the period in which he has to wear it: '(the Father) seems to set him apart only in actual operation because of the human flesh which he wears – (Marcellus means that the Son was differentiated only by what he did, not by what he was) – and appoints him apparently a certain fixed period consisting of the session at the right hand' (II,3,7 (51)). A little later he argues: 'Now if anyone says that human flesh is worthy of the Word on the grounds that he has rendered it immortal by means of the resurrection, he should realize that not everything, just because it is immortal, is thereby worthy of God' (II,4,13–14 (52)). In the next section Eusebius quotes a passage from Marcellus which contains a very salutary reminder that we know very little about the nature of Christ's resurrection body: 'We do not think it safe to make dogmatic pronouncements about matters concerning which we have no clear teaching in the sacred scriptures.' Eusebius concludes his review of Marcellus' teaching with a protest that, according to Marcellus, at the parousia a humanity which is immortal, divine, incorruptible, and indestructible, will be left on its own. He comments: 'Surely without the Word the body will be left alone in a condition of immortal and incorruptible irrationality (*alogia* – is this a pun?) and inertia' (II,4,23–24 (54)).

Marcellus' own position was no doubt indefensible. The early church could not do without a doctrine of the Logos as a distinct *hypostasis*. But he certainly posed very acutely the problem of the body, and indeed the humanity of the risen Christ. The fact that Gregory of Nyssa could accept so much of his conclusions proves this.

We turn then to Gregory of Nyssa, and reproduce first a passage in which he deals directly with the problem of the Lord's body during the *triduum*; it comes from a sermon *De Triduo Spatio*:

> How can the Lord be at the same time in paradise and in Hades? One solution of the problem is to say that nothing is impossible for God in whom all things hold together. Another solution, to which our argument now leads is this: God transforms the entire humanity, by means of its being associated with him, into the divine nature, so that during the period of the divine dispensation of the passion it was not the case that one element, having been fused with God then separated itself (seeing that the gifts of God are without repentance); but rather that the godhead deliberately dissociated the soul from the body, but manifested itself as still abiding in both. For by means of the body, in which it could not suffer the corruption of death, it foiled him who has the power of death; but by means of the soul it gave to the robber access to paradise. Thus both events operate at the same time, while the godhead brings about a good result by each: by the incorruption of the body the destruction of death is brought about, and the entry of men into paradise by means of the soul gravitating towards its natural habitat.[13]

This is neat and ingenious, though it is difficult to resist the impression that we are playing an elaborate game with counters rather than dealing with realities. We note the tendency to divinize and thereby spiritualize the risen body.

Later on Gregory represents the risen Christ as saying to the women: 'Do not touch me – in this mean and servile guise of humanity, for I am not yet ascended to the glory of the Father.'[14] This probably suggests a glorified humanity rather than no humanity at all. But in a sermon on the Ascension,[15] he imagines Christ ascending into heaven and being challenged by the heavenly hosts in the words of Psalm 24: 'Who is this king of glory?' Gregory comments 'because he bears the sordid garment of our life, the redness of whose clothes comes from the winepress of human sufferings, he is not recognized'. So we must understand the process of glorification of the body as not having taken place until Christ actually entered heaven. So that the Lord apparently rose with a body that was incorruptible because of its association with the Logos, but one which had not yet been glorified.

So far Gregory has not advanced beyond a position which is common to many of the Greek Fathers. But he certainly went well beyond this. R. M. Hübner points out that, in his account of the ultimate state of all things after the parousia Gregory makes use of two strictly incompatible concepts;[16] the first was the idea that all mankind would ultimately be incorporated in the body of Christ. This idea he got from Marcellus of Ancyra. The other idea was that ultimately the whole creation, including the angelic creation, would be included in the body of Christ. This came from Origen, and it was this idea that prevailed in Gregory's thought. At times therefore when Gregory writes of the body of Christ he means simply the whole of human nature. Hübner maintains that 'the principle of this saved humanity is Christ the God-man, not the Logos'.[17] On the other hand Gregory interpreted the parable of the lost sheep so as to make the one lost sheep represent fallen humanity and the ninety-nine that were not lost represent the angels. When therefore humanity is reconciled to God in Christ, it shares in a spiritual, angelic nature.[18] Similarly he interprets Psalm 150.5 'Praise God with the clash of cymbals' as indicating 'the unity of our nature with that of the angels'. 'In the end time', he writes, 'one cymbal is the supermundane nature of the angels, the other is the spiritual creation (= creatures) of men'.[19]

But in another respect it was Marcellus rather than Origen who had the last word with Gregory. In several passages he maintains that the end condition of the all must be the same as the aboriginal state, i.e. that in the end everything will have been in some sense to become Spirit. Thus, in a sermon on I Cor. 15.28 he writes: 'The divine Word possessed the Father's glory before the world was: since in the fullness of time he became flesh, the flesh by its contact with the Word had to become that which the Word is. So the flesh comes to receive that which the Word possessed before the world existed. But that is the Holy Spirit.'[20] Again: 'Christ must always be the same both before the dispensation (of the incarnation) and afterwards. But he was man neither beforehand nor after it, but only in the period of the dispensation'.[21] Gregory is therefore no champion of a pre-existent humanity. In his *Commentary on the Song of Songs*, writing of the eschatological state, he says: 'all shall be one body and one Spirit'. Hübner comments: 'The process whereby human nature becomes the body is a process of becoming spirit',[22] and maintains vigorously as against Harnack and others that Gregory did not envisage the process of final salvation for all spiritual natures as being a physical one, though he describes it on the model of a physical process.[23] And we may quote one final comment from Hübner which sums up Gregory's position clearly: 'An analysis of the final state of the body of Christ . . . shows clearly that the ultimate principle of the unity of the body is Christ's godhead and that his manhood has no further significance'.[24]

So Gregory offers us a very plain example of a Greek theologian who has in effect disposed altogether of the risen body of Christ as far as its being a body is concerned. He has in effect spiritualized it away completely.

Before considering Augustine, we might mention a remarkable passage from Jerome quoted by Darwell Stone:

> But the blood of Christ and the flesh of Christ are to be understood in two ways. There is that spiritual and divine flesh and blood of which he says 'My flesh is truly food, and my blood is truly drink', and 'Except ye shall have eaten my flesh and drunk my blood, ye shall not have eternal life'. There is also the flesh which was crucified and the blood which flowed from the wound made by the soldier's lance. According to this distinction a difference of flesh and blood is understood also in the case of his saints, so that there is one flesh which will see the salvation of God, and there is another flesh and blood which cannot possess the kingdom of God.[25]

Here is a Latin Father (no doubt under the influence of Origen) tending to spiritualize the body. On the other hand in Theodoret of Cyrrnus we have a Greek Father (admittedly an Antiochene) who takes a traditionally Western view. In Dialogue 2 he argues with a Eutychian heretic who held that 'after the ascension the body of Christ is changed into the divine nature so as to be no longer a human body'. Theodoret maintains on the contrary that 'after the ascension the body of Christ still remains a human body, although it is now incorruptible and glorious'.[26]

Augustine's position on this question is very interesting, since he saw clearly the impossibility of maintaining that the physical body of the risen Lord could be available to the faithful. He therefore clearly distinguished the humanity of the Word, which was in heaven, from his eternal divinity, which of course shared all the properties of God and was available for us. The body which ascended, he said, is not made of spirit, but is subjected to spirit; and he very reasonably adds that we cannot know, and should not try to discover, 'where and in what manner the Lord's body is in heaven'.[27] He distinguishes the omnipresence of Christ as God from his restricted presence as man: 'who is it that is seated at the right hand of the Father? The man Christ'.[28] Both he and Ambrose insist that Christ as man is in heaven and is not to be sought or found on earth.[29] And Augustine regarded with apprehension the spiritualizing school. He writes: 'we must beware of so deifying the manhood as to do away with the reality of the body'.[30] In Sermon 361 he gives a very clear classification of the various modes of Christ's presence, as follows: (1) He is present in glory, eternally united with the Father. (2) In his bodily presence he is above the heavens at the Father's right hand. (3) In his presence of faith he is in all Christians.[31] Augustine is not willing to confer a unique ubiquity on Christ's risen body, as John Scotus Erigena and Luther did later. 'Present in all things inasmuch as he is God, he is on the other hand in heaven inasmuch as he is man.'[32]

In her book *Augustine on the Body*, Margaret Miles has traced the evolution of Augustine's thought on this question.[33] He began from a Platonic emphasis on the immortality of the soul. He believed in the resurrection of the body, but saw no connection between our mortal bodies and our resurrection bodies. In AD 393 he was teaching that the parousia brings us an *immutatio angelica*: what is raised is 'body' but not 'flesh'.[34] By the end of his life he was holding that we will ultimately in some sense see God with the eyes of our flesh. The resurrection body will be continuous with the mortal body. He used the example of Jesus' risen body to illuminate the nature of our risen bodies – which is exactly what we today cannot do with conviction. The *corpus spirituale* does not become spirit, but is penetrated and directed by spirit. This applies also, of course, to Christ's risen body: it followed that Christ's glorified body in heaven was the same as it was when he ascended into heaven. It therefore possesses bones and flesh.[35]

We should also note another element in the Fathers' teaching about the significance of the risen body, well exemplified in Chrysostom's claim that through the ascension of Christ into heaven the Father received the first-fruits of our nature.[36] This certainly gave more meaning to the doctrine, since it associated it with the ultimate destiny of the faithful. It is based, of course, on Paul's concept of Christ as the 'first-fruits of those who have fallen asleep' (I Cor. 15.20). But Paul was thinking in terms of the parousia: our condition then was to be like Christ's now. It is by no means clear that Paul would have drawn the conclusion which subsequent Christian thinkers drew that 'humanity is seated on the throne of the universe'.

Before leaving the Fathers, we may relevantly glance at what John of Damascus has to say on the subject. It is interesting to observe that he accepts the notion of a pre-existent manhood; in his *Exposition of the Orthodox Faith* he writes: 'the Son of Man is allowed to have been in heaven before the passion', and he quotes John 3.13.[37] It also looks as if the doctrine of a double consciousness, a divine and a human, belonging to the incarnate Word is to be prolonged into eternity: at III,21,68 we learn that the Word took the ignorance of humanity, but his humanity was enriched with knowledge of the future by means of the divine Word, and that this continues in the post-resurrection state. In IV,1,74, we have a clear statement of the condition of the ascended Lord. At his ascension 'he laid aside none of the divisions of his nature, neither body nor spirit, but possesses both the body and the soul intelligent and reasonable, volitional and energetic, and in this wise he sits at the right hand of the Father, using his will both as God and as man on behalf of our salvation'. And again: 'Christ sits in the body at the right hand of the Father in actual place . . . we understand the right hand of the Father to be the glory and honour of the godhead in which the Son of God . . . has a seat in the body, his flesh sharing in the glory' (IV,2,74).

With the development of eucharistic theology another purpose was found for the Lord's risen body. John of Damascus, for example, proclaims the actual identity of the eucharistic elements with the body and blood of the Lord.[38] His contemporary who lived at the other end of Europe, Bede, describes the ascension as the ground of the sacraments. Using an analogy found elsewhere in the Fathers, he says that as Elijah left his cloak behind him when he ascended, so the glorified Christ has left us the sacraments.[39] This doctrine, of course, underwent a very considerable development in the West and proved to be a burning theological issue at the Reformation. Indeed it would not be an exaggeration to say that the doctrine of the risen humanity of the Word was only needed by the church for two purposes: to assure the faithful of the hope of a risen life after death, and to connect the eucharistic elements (much more the bread than the wine) with the risen Christ. This second purpose created a number of difficulties on its own, quite apart from the problem of how a finite humanity can be reconciled with an infinite divine purpose.

Thomas Aquinas deals with the question of the risen humanity of Christ in his customary lucid and magisterial way. He had of course inherited a doctrine of the presence of Christ's body in the eucharist which he proceeded to interpret according to the familiar Aristotelian categories. But this need not concern us now. What is of interest is the clear manner in which he distinguishes between the availability of the divinity and the unavailability of the humanity. He concludes that Christ rose from the dead with his real body, but it was able to go through closed doors because of the divinity to which it belonged.[40] But he adds that the capacity to appear or disappear may also belong to the bodies of defunct saints. He also suggests that since the risen body was spiritual (and he quotes I Cor. 15.44), it was altogether subject to the Spirit and therefore could behave as it did.[41] He believes that Christ's risen body was a glorified one, and in this respect different from the condition, though not from the nature, of the pre-resurrection body. He quotes Gregory the Great: 'the body of Christ after the resurrection is shown to have been of the same nature but of a different degree of glory' (*alterius gloriae*). Remarkably Thomas resists any suggestion that the Lord's body was divinized during the period of the incarnation, thereby differing from the Eastern Orthodox tradition.[42] The risen body possessed flesh, bones and blood, and all other properties of a natural body, miraculously preserved from corruption.[43]

Thomas has no doubt but that the risen body is in a place, though he distinguishes it from the sort of place we know: 'The place (*locus*) in which we live is a place of generation and corruption; but the heavenly place is a place of incorruption'.[44] And he makes a very important distinction between the risen humanity of the Word and his divinity: 'Although the corporal presence of Christ was withdrawn from the faithful by the ascension, nevertheless the presence of his divinity is always there for the faithful.' And he adds: 'Because Christ located his assumed human nature in heaven, he gave us a hope of arriving there'.[45]

When he deals with the heavenly session, Thomas is very circumspect indeed. He obviously does not want to confine it to the risen humanity alone, as he says that sitting at the right hand of God must not be taken in a literal or local sense. It means eternal beatitude and kingly power.[46] We can say that Christ sits at the right hand of God as man in the sense that his human nature is filled with the greatest possible grace and beatitude, and in virtue of the fact that it possesses the power and right to judge all other human creatures.[47]

Thomas Aquinas thus neatly exemplifies the position of traditional Western theology on this question: with the important exceptions of the hope of the faithful and the nature of the consecrated elements in the eucharist, he virtually has no use for the risen humanity of the Word. Apart from the eucharist, we have no access to it. Therefore it cannot be generally available to the faithful. The problem of how the consecrated elements in the eucharist can be identified with the risen body of Christ (and this in turn with his body crucified for us) is one which we must consider later on. We shall find that it remains a very difficult problem indeed. What is important to observe now is that, apart from the eucharist, the risen body of Christ remained an intractable problem for traditional Christian theology. The doctrine of hypostatic union, far from helping to resolve the problem, was actually instrumental in creating it.

The status of the risen body of Christ presented a special problem to the Reformers. They all, with one consent, rejected the doctrine of transubstantiation. But this doctrine, however unintelligible it may seem to us moderns, did give what appeared to be a comprehensible account of how the body of Christ could be at one and the same time in heaven and present on our altars at the eucharist. The Reformers had to find an alternative explanation. As we have seen, Luther fell back on John Scotus Erigena's doctrine of the ubiquity of the Lord's risen body. It could be in more than one place at the same time. This did not mean that Luther could dispense with a local heaven for the place where the body is. For example, he actually maintained that the intercession of the risen Lord in his body in heaven was *oralis et realis*, he 'orally and actually' interceded for us in heaven, an astonishing piece of literalism.[48] Calvin more moderately accepted *realis* but not *oralis*. Tait severely criticizes Luther for such literalism: 'To allege that

because Christ is omnipotent as God therefore his body is also omnipresent is to predicate of the humanity properties which belong only to
the deity.' He adds, as if uneasily aware that such a practice was quite
usual among theologians: 'The hypostatic union permits, it is true, the
interchange of language, commonly known as *communicatio idiomatum*,
but interchange of the essential properties of the two natures would
involve the nullifying of both.'[49] When we come to discuss Tait's own
treatment of the problem, we shall see that he is certainly not in a
position to criticize Luther in this respect, and his reference to the
communicatio idiomatum is an admission that in fact the orthodox christology itself, which of course he defends, was by no means free of the
sort of verbal *leger de main* of which he accuses Luther. It is amusing
(for an Anglican at least) to observe that Luther's doctrine of the
ubiquity of the risen Lord's body is by no means out-dated, for it is
espoused by none other than the radical unmetaphysical Moltmann
today. He writes: 'He [Christ] is also, according to his humanity,
bodily present in the divine presence that permeates all things.' He
adds that we have fellowship 'with the crucified Jesus, his body given
on Golgotha and his blood shed there, not with any heavenly body of
Christ'.[50] It seems to me either that this is meaningless rhetoric or that
Moltmann does not intend us to take him literally, but is really describing a spiritual relationship.

Calvin began from Augustine's position, and spoke of a risen body
in a localized, spatial heaven: 'Inasmuch as he is God, he is in all
things; inasmuch as he is man, he is in heaven.'[51] Calvin is actually
quoting Augustine here. When faced with the problem of how to
explain Christ's body in the eucharist, Calvin with great acuteness fell
back on the doctrine of the Holy Spirit. But we shall be considering
this more carefully later. Tait's comment on Calvin is just: 'Calvin
admits that (philosophically speaking) there is no place above the skies
but, since the body of Christ, bearing the nature and mode of a human
body, is finite and contained in heaven as its place, Christ's session *at
the right hand of God* necessarily signifies the local separation of the body
from the earth.'[52]

The other Reformers tend to follow Calvin rather than Luther.
Cranmer maintained that corporally Christ is in heaven but spiritually
he is with all believers everywhere. Hooker claims that 'the body of
Christ, seated at the right hand of God, is as truly human as it was upon

earth', and emphatically repudiates the conception that Christ as man is omnipresent.[53] The matter is expressed with admirable lucidity in Article XXXI of the Thirty-Nine Articles:

> Forasmuch as the truth of man's nature requires that it cannot be at the same time in many places but in some certain and fixed place, therefore the body of Christ cannot be present at the same time in many and divers places. And because, as Holy Scripture doth teach, Christ was taken up into heaven, and will there remain until the end of the world, no-one of the faithful ought either to believe or openly to confess the real and bodily presence, as they term it, of his flesh and blood in the eucharist.

Those who have seen the film version of Brecht's play *Galileo* will remember the scene in which Galileo explains to a friend in Venice the implications of his discovery that there are moons orbiting Jupiter: the planets and the earth must be floating freely in space. The friend, horrified, exclaims 'But if so, where is God?' This exclamation might come appropriately enough from a dedicated Aristotelian, but the appropriate reaction of the Christian theologian might well have been rather: 'Where is Christ's risen body?' One does not gain the impression that the sixteenth-century Reformers were much worried about the new astronomy, probably because they lived before Galileo had confirmed and publicized Copernicus' theory. But the theory of a heliocentric universe certainly made it more difficult to say where Christ's risen body could be. However, old beliefs die hard. As late as 1874 and 1890 an English divine could insist that, since it is the humanity of Christ that triumphs and intercedes, there must be an actual throne somewhere in heaven and oral intercession must continually take place there.[54]

The Tractarians had no intention of innovating in this area. We find Keble writing in 1858: 'With that body and blood [previously defined as 'his glorious body with all its wounds'] he [Christ] appears continually before the throne.'[55] Keble, however, does seem to be aware that he is moving in difficult country, for he adds: 'as the divine Word or Person of Christ is everywhere and always present and adorable, so ever since the incarnation the presence of the body of Christ, or the presence of the soul of Christ, or of both united whenever and wherever and however he wills to notify it, is to be taken as a warrant and call for especial adoration. There is just a hint in that word 'however,' that there could be a difficulty about the ubiquity of the body and soul of Christ. But E. B. Pusey, writing in 1867, asserts quite straight-forwardly that Christ is 'locally present in his natural body at the right hand of the Father'.[56]

This makes it all the more surprising that Anglicans, writing either late in the nineteenth or actually in the twentieth century, could still use so much of the language of traditional orthodoxy about the risen humanity of the Word. The great B. F. Westcott was a scholar who was prepared to use the methods of biblical criticism as known in his day, but this did not prevent him from treating the resurrection narratives very much as if they were records of fully historical reliability. He writes of the risen body of Christ 'He can obey at his will the present laws of material being, but he is not bound by them.' Again 'the change which Christ revealed by the ascension was not a change of place, but a change of state, not local but spiritual.' This is, of course, a concession to the astronomy of his day, but it does not make it any easier to say what is then meant by the risen body of Christ, and even Westcott's concession that 'we are entered into fellowship with a world in which human standards of time have no place' is somewhat inadequate as an explanation.[57]

In H. B. Swete we have a champion of traditional christology who devoted a whole volume to the subject of the ascension. Though no believer in the verbal inspiration of scripture, his approach to the resurrection narratives is very conservative by the standards of today. He writes: 'the resurrection had placed the flesh of the Word so far under the control of the Spirit that his body, as the Gospels show, was, even before the ascension, independent when he so willed, of the laws that govern matter'.[58] And again 'in the depths of his divine consciousness the Son of Man had memories of the glory which in his pre-incarnate life he had *with the Father before the world was.* . . . But the human soul of Christ, up to the moment of the ascension, had had no experience of the full vision of God which burst upon it when he was taken up.' Quite apart from the assumption that John 17 is literal reportage, this sentence seems to assume that the double consciousness which the traditional christology so often takes for granted in the incarnate Word continues in the risen Christ after the ascension. We can well sympathize with those of the Fathers such as Origen and Hilary who were anxious to spiritualize and in effect nullify the human nature of the Lord after the ascension. A double consciousness during the period of the incarnation is sufficiently hard to justify without prolonging it into eternity, as Swete seems to do.

Later on Swete becomes more explicit about how he envisages the risen humanity as operating: 'Even in his earthly humiliation the incarnate Word manifested unique power over nature', and he speaks of 'superhuman' powers. He follows this up by asking: 'what limit shall be put to the glorified manhood?' – he means in controlling nature.[59] But he himself has already claimed that in the days of his flesh Christ's power over nature came from the divinity, not the humanity. Westcott is quoted as saying that the ascension is 'the enlargement of his [Christ's] human capacities to a degree that we cannot measure, and it carries with it a corresponding increase of the content of his consciousness and of the exercise of his power'. Once again we encounter the strange implication that the divine Word carried a double consciousness into the eternal sphere. What is the point of positing a humanity, however enlarged and divinized, in a sphere where, in effect, only divinity can operate? The human nature of the Word, once the resurrection-ascension has taken place, becomes nothing but an embarrassment, except as concerns our relation to the risen Lord after death. Some further light is gained when we read: 'the glorified humanity is, as far as manhood can be this, a perfect medium for the self-expression of the divine Word. The personal force which lies behind the forces of nature . . . works through the human mind and will of the ascended Christ, so far as the human in its perfected state is said to respond to the divine.'[60] There is some truth here, in the sense that the risen Christ is the form and image in which Christians know God the Word, as I hope to show in a later chapter. But it seems to be nothing but an embarrassment and a complication to insist that somewhere in the eternal realm the humanity of Christ is operating as an instrument for God's dealings with the universe and with men. Certainly as far as God's relation to the forces of nature is concerned Christ's humanity would be nothing but an impediment. And even in the relation of the divine Word with Christians the fact that humanity is a finite entity would seem to disqualify it from playing any mediatorial rôle. This is not to disparage the central importance of the incarnation, as I hope to show; but the embarrassment for Christian theology caused by having to find a place for the substantial humanity of the Word in the post-resurrection period does not decrease but rather increases in the light of modern cosmology.

Swete comes to the traditional conclusion about the place of the risen Christ when he writes: 'Man sits in Jesus Christ on the throne of God, and in him the race has a "daysman" betwixt itself and God who can "lay his hand on both".'[61] The quotation from Job 9.33 is unfortunate, since Job is asking for someone who is neither God nor man, someone in fact much more like the Arian Christ, or Philo's Logos. The function of the divine Word is not to arbitrate between God and man, but to bring God to man because he is God and has uniquely spoken by means of the man Jesus Christ. But the statement that man sits on the throne of God actually does not seem to mean anything. The incomprehensibility of the concept of the Word's humanity continuing to operate in the post-resurrection period is a direct correlate of the incomprehensibility of the concept of hypostatic union, if by that is meant God actually becoming identical with one of us.

Although he writes later than both Westcott and Swete, Tait does not seem to be able to advance very much further than they did. He quotes Swete: 'While the sacred humanity retains all that is essential to human nature, it must needs be free from all conditions of space.'[62] We have already learned from Westcott that in considering the risen body human standards of time (which are, after all, the only standards we possess) have no place. It is very difficult therefore to find any meaning left for the phrase 'the risen humanity'. Tait concludes that, in order to make sense of their conceptions, both Westcott and Swete require that Christ's humanity 'be rendered capable of omnipresence',[63] but he (very wisely) ends his chapter on a note of reverent agnosticism. By the end of his book[64] he has committed himself both to the proposition (accepted by both Westcott and Swete) that the ascension was a change of state not of place, and that heaven must be thought of as a state rather than as a place. In other words, Tait has realized the intellectual impasse into which the traditional doctrine of the risen humanity of the Word has run, but instead of re-examining his premises he prefers to fall back on agnosticism as far as this subject is concerned.

Before going on to the moderns, we should pay some attention to two Anglican theologians of the same period as Swete and Tait who seem to show a greater affinity with Origen and Gregory of Nyssa on this subject, than with the Western tradition. The first is Charles Gore who wrote in his book *The Body of Christ* of 1901; 'The risen body of Christ is spiritual ... not because it was less than before material, but because in it matter was wholly and finally subjugated to spirit and not to the exigencies of physical life ... As to what "the body of glory" is, silence is our best wisdom.'[65] R. M. Benson, writing in 1907, goes further:

> People talk of Christ's body as if it were the body of any other man. They do not realise that it is ascended to the right hand of God. They think of Christ sitting in heaven as he may be represented in a picture with the form which he might have had during his earthly life. They do not realise what is meant by ascension. He did not ascend to some place in the sky miles and miles away from earth. He ascended by passing up from an earthly form of existence, measured by space and outline, to an entirely new sphere and manner and capacity of life. He ascended up a little way above the heads of the bystanders, and then he vanished out of their sight. . . . He was crucified in a natural body. He rose again as a spiriutal body. That spiritual body is incapable of any earthly measurement or form. It is a heavenly power such as we can in no wise apprehend. . . . It is no longer in space, but it is at the right hand of God exercising a power by the inherent glory of the Holy Ghost. It is no longer in space, but it acts independently of space, so that however many may be the altars on which the Holy Eucharist is celebrated, there is no multiplication of Christ's body. His body, being now a spiritual body, is a force divinely operating in every crumb of the consecrated bread, communicating the existence of its glorified state to each one who feeds thereon.[66]

This is Origenistic spiritualizing and not Lutheran ubiquitarianism.

We should also look at J. G. Davies account of the risen humanity, which he gives us at the end of his valuable work on the history of the doctrine of the ascension, so often quoted already. He writes: 'His [Christ's] body, glorified through resurrection and ascension, is now the centre and substance of his mystical body, the church – hence the virtual identity between them.'[67] We are in deep water here, for certainly Paul closely associates Christ's risen body with the church. But to use the words 'centre and substance' is dangerous. In view, for example, of E. Schweizer's article *sōma* in the *Theologisches Wörterbuch zum Neuen Testament*,[68] it would be more accurate to use the word 'area of existence', and surely the rôle which the Spirit plays in Paul's thought at this point should not be omitted. And the phrase 'virtual identity' would be challenged by many Pauline scholars. J. G. Davies differs from his Anglican predecessors of fifty years before in the fact that he does not insist too dogmatically on the historical nature of the ascension. He regards it as primarily a symbol for the return of Christ to the Father. Unlike Westcott and Swete, he does not suggest that a double consciousness persisted in the divine Word after the ascension, though he seems to hold that it existed up to the time of the ascension: 'what is involved in this reformulation of the (kenotic) theory is a limitation of consciousness rather than of actual being'.[69] At the ascension, he writes: 'the manhood . . . entered upon a new mode of being, and was liberated from its previous limitations'. Here we are once again in the impasse to which, it seems, Westcott and Swete were reduced: in what way was the *manhood* limited during the period of the incarnation? If anything, it was the divinity that was limited then. Why then does the manhood need 'liberating' after the ascension? Only, we must conclude, so that it can be turned into something quite different, an omnipresent manhood, surely a contradiction in terms. Then we read: 'Henceforth the Second Hypostasis of the godhead is divine humanity.'[70] If this is taken literally, it means that the humanity has actually replaced the divinity in the Word, which is certainly not Davies' meaning. In fact, it seems to imply a sort of post-resurrection Monophysitism. This reminds us of John Cassian's opinion already quoted,[71] which Tait characterizes as 'a species of monophysitism'.[72] Davies' final word is that the manhood of Christ (by which he means the manhood eternally belonging to the divine Word) 'provides the point of contact between God and us in our creaturely state'.[73] This, it seems to me, is precisely what it cannot do. And the bulk of the Western tradition, including Augustine and Aquinas, have been careful to state that it is the divinity, and not the humanity of the risen Lord that is the means by which he is related to us, always excepting the question of the eucharist, which we must reserve for later consideration. I do not know whether J. G. Davies has changed his views on christology since he published his study of the doctrine of the ascension in 1958. Many of us have during the past twenty years. But as they stand in this

book they do not seem to have come to terms with the genuine difficulties inherent in the traditional theology which he espouses.

We now turn to a great continental theologian, to examine what he
has to say about the nature of the risen humanity of the Word and its
relation to us. As a matter of fact, it is not very easy to pin-point this
subject in the huge area of Karl Barth's *Church Dogmatics*,[74] but as far
as my researches go I can only find relevant material in two volumes
of the *Dogmatics*, III, 2 and IV, 2. I shall be quoting indiscriminately
from both without necessarily observing Barth's own order of topics.

I begin with a very explicit statement by Barth of how he understands the doctrine of hypostatic union.[75] He rejects a whole series of
analogies for the nature of this union: it is not consubstantial, as is
that of the persons of the Trinity (despite Chalcedon's 'of one substance with us as regards his manhood'); it is not the same sort of
relationship as that whereby God maintains all things in existence; it
is not analogous to any union between two human beings; it is not
like a man in a suit of clothes, or in a coat; it can find no analogy in
philosophy, e.g. that of form and matter; Barth also rejects the analogy
of soul and body in man (despite the patronage of both Augustine and
Calvin), because in that analogy each needs the other; the analogy of
the Lord's presence in the eucharist will not do for that would cast the
church itself in the rôle of a kind of prolongation of the incarnation.
Last of all Karl Barth rejects the analogy of the indwelling of the Holy
Spirit in the sanctified. In this connection he mentions D. M. Baillie's
book *God was in Christ* to which much reference has already been
made in this work. Most unfortunately, however, instead of answering
Baillie's arguments directly, he associates him with a continental
theologian of the last century (E. E. Biedermann, 1885) and contents
himself with answering Biedermann. As Biedermann's christology was
deeply integrated with Hegelian philosophy, what will suffice to
answer him will by no means provide a fair reply to Baillie. Barth
admits that Baillie was not 'guilty of the flagrant extravagances of
Biedermann', but that is little comfort. We are left with the conclusion
that there can be no analogy at all for the nature of the hypostatic
union, and hence presumably that the question: 'how was Jesus God
and man?' must remain to a very large extent a mystery. He goes on to
describe Jesus' being Son of God as being 'participator in the divine
essence', and says that this was given to Jesus 'by divine grace'. This

might seem a step towards Baillie (though Augustine could say this)[76] but the phrase 'divine essence' is hardly compatible with Baillie's view. Moreover Barth has already explicitly adopted the doctrine that the human nature of the Word was *anhypostatos*: 'In Jesus Christ it is not merely one man, but the *humanum* of all men, which is posited and exalted as such to unity with God.' He actually uses the word *anhypostasia*.[77]

Next we should take note of a remarkable doctrine of Barth's whereby he claims that in some sense the humanity of Jesus Christ was pre-existent. We first get a hint of this in the statement from III, 2: 'The life of Jesus begins, and therefore it was once future. But the man Jesus already was even before he was.'[78] This is then repeated: 'Jesus, as the Word of God, as the real basis of creation'; and 'the man Jesus was . . . already at the beginning of time as the One who was to come in the plan of God'.[79] In IV, 2 Barth claims that the whole of the Prologue to the Fourth Gospel ('with the possible exception of the first phrase of v. 1') 'speaks also of the man Jesus', and he refers to John 8.28. He immediately makes the same claim for Hebrews on the basis of Heb. 1.4.[80] It is quite true that Paul and the author of the Epistle to the Hebrews do sometimes imply that the name Jesus Christ can be applied to the pre-existent being who became incarnate in Jesus of Nazareth, but this is probably because they had no agreed terminology for pre-existence. It is very different with John, and I should be inclined to deny that John does use Jesus Christ of the pre-existent Word. I discuss this question more fully in a later chapter, but we should note that Karl Barth's doctrine of pre-existence assumes not just the pre-existence of the divine Word, but of the divine Word existing in some (non-incarnate) mode as man and as therefore bearing the name Jesus Christ long before the historical character Jesus of Nazareth appeared on the scene. This seems to me to have no certain warrant in scripture, and to add an unnecessary and incredible element to the doctrine of the incarnation. We meet something very like it however presently in C. F. D. Moule, and must give it careful consideration later.[81]

Barth does discuss the nature of the resurrection appearances, according to them a historical character that few modern scholars would defend. He says that it was during the forty days between the resurrection and the ascension that the disciples recognized Jesus unmistakably as God, a conclusion which most students of the development of christology in the early church would probably regard as rash.[82] Barth shows a tendency to try to avoid stressing too much the 'corporeality' of the accounts of the resurrection appearances in the gospels, which suggests that he is aware of the difficulty of explaining what exactly is meant by the 'glorified humanity' or the 'exaltation of the risen body to the side of God'.[83] But he treats all four gospels as being on a level as far as evidence for the resurrection appearances (or indeed anything else), is concerned. This is shown by his reference to Peter's walking on the water in Matt. 14.29 as if it was historical.[84] In fact one must conclude that Barth was not prepared to allow a critical approach to the resurrection narratives to interfere with his dogmatic conclusions.

It follows, therefore, that when Barth comes to state what is the nature of the risen Lord, he is as uninhibited by his belief in the exaltation of the humanity of the Word as any of the theologians whom we have just been considering: 'Between his (Jesus') death and his resurrection there is a transformation, but no alteration, division, or least of all subtraction'.[85] This in itself would be unexceptionable. But he applies exactly the same sentiment to the exalted Word. A little later he writes: 'the man Jesus was manifested to them (the disciples) in the *mode* of God',[86] which chimes in with his claim that it was then that the disciples unmistakably recognized him as God. He also writes that Christ ascended as man and is now sharing God's throne and after Easter 'the man Jesus is but transcendentally present'.[87] In IV, 2 Barth is more specific on this subject. Of the eternal Son's relation to his assumed humanity he writes: 'As he adopts it, making it his own existence in his divine nature, he does not deify it, but he exalts it into the *consortium divinitatis*, into an inward and indestructible fellowship with his godhead, which he does not in any degree surrender or forfeit, but supremely maintains, when he becomes man'.[88] He adds on the next page that there is therefore no 'knowledge of God which can escape his humanity', and he goes on to identify this with human nature once for all definitely exalted in Jesus Christ'. Again he states that after the ascension Jesus Christ was 'placed as man at the side of God', and 'He lives this high and true and royal human life which corresponds to his divine Sonship'.[89]

We may readily agree with Karl Barth when he says that we now know God in Christ but this does not necessarily require a doctrine of the exaltation of the humanity in the throne of God which runs a grave risk of reducing theology to a series of fine-sounding but meaningless statements. What does it mean to say that Jesus Christ is 'placed as man at the side of God'? How can humanity share the throne of the universe? Barth never tackles this question. Still less does he say what it means to claim that the risen Lord has a body eternally in heaven. Barth does not even go as far as Tait did in 1912 and introduce a saving element of reverent agnosticism.

In the discussion of the previous theologians of the orthodox tradition we noted two problems which have to be faced. The first is the nature of the exalted body of Christ's humanity. On this, as we have seen, we gain little light from Barth. The second was the relation of the exalted humanity to the faithful. Not very much is to be gleaned on this topic either from the *Church Dogmatics*, but we may observe this passage: 'But in this second form (the first is the Word's existence as eternal Son) his relationship to his body the community *is* the relationship of God and man as it takes place in this one Being as head and body. Thus the community of Jesus Christ can be that which the human nature of its Lord and head is.'[90] Does this not mean that the mode in which God the Word dwells in us *is* Jesus Christ's human nature? But that is meaningless. What else does our relation to God in Christ mean but that God can dwell in us in some way analogous to that in which he dwelt in Jesus Christ? Indeed this analogy is explicitly drawn out in the latter half of John 17. We think also of those passages both in Paul and Hebrews where Jesus Christ is presented as archetypal believer, even in some places (e.g. Heb. 5.7–10) as the paradigm of the individual undergoing salvation. Barth's determination to hold on to an essentialist or ontological union between Jesus and the Word, and to prolong this union into the dimension of eternity, would seem to have brought him perilously near to sheer meaninglessness, and even to have blinded him to some important elements in New Testament christology.

We have already noticed that Karl Barth definitely repudiates the Eastern Orthodox doctrine that the indwelling of the Logos had the effect of divinizing the humanity of the incarnate Word, though there is one point where he might seem to be moving in that direction. In III, 2 he writes: 'For Jesus does not have the Spirit in the way in which it can be said of any man that he has the Spirit. . . . This is his absolutely unique relationship to the Holy Spirit.'[91] Paul would certainly have agreed with this as far as the risen life of Christ is concerned, but he would not have applied it to the incarnate life as well, as Barth apparently does. Shortly afterwards Barth suggests that because of this unique relation to the Spirit, Jesus' flesh was from the beginning destined to salvation – prèsumably in a manner that ours cannot be. This distinguishes the humanity of the Word from ours in a way which might form the basis for a theory of divinization.[92] It is not, apparently, merely the sinlessness of Jesus that constitutes this unique relation to the Spirit. However, apart from the passage from IV, 2 already referred to,[93] there are two other passages where Barth repudiates the notion of any such divinization: in the first[94] he describes the risen Jesus as 'the Son of Man who is not divinised but exalted to the side of God'. And in the second, he specifically rejects the notion of divinization.[95] What he does not explain, of course, is how the human nature can be exalted to the side of God without undergoing divinization.

It must be said that Karl Barth's treatment of the theme of the risen humanity is disappointing. For the most part he is content to repeat the well-worn formulae about the humanity being exalted to the side of God without explaining what he means by this. To some extent he may even be accused of evading the issue about the risen body in a way which Westcott, Swete, and Tait do not. They, at any rate, provided some sort of a solution, Westcott and Swete by an unacknowledged doctrine of the ubiquity of the humanity, Tait by an acknowledged agnosticism. Barth does not even seem to admit that the problem exists. In addition he introduces a difficult concept of the pre-existence of Jesus as man which does not seem to have much basis in traditional christology, and which, though it can appeal to some apparent support in the New Testament, only serves to complicate and unnecessarily obscure doctrines which are, even at their clearest, in urgent need of presentation in terms intelligible to moderns. It cannot be said that Karl Barth has even attempted to do this, still less succeeded in doing so.

I have already referred to G. Martelet's valuable work on the eucharist in my discussion of Augustine, and I shall be turning to it again when we come to consider the eucharistic presence of the Word. Here we may content ourselves with a brief examination of Martelet's treatment of the risen body of Christ, and its general relation to Christians. Christ's resurrection, he says, is transformation of the body. The resurrection appearances, which he treats in a rather conservative manner, fit in with 'the profound paradox of a "spiritual body" ',[96] and he calls the ascension 'the end of the economic phase of the appearances'. But he does not deal with the difficulty that Paul, our earliest written witness to belief in the resurrection, appears to regard the appearance of the risen Christ to him as being on a par with the other resurrection appearances.

However, despite a rather literalistic treatment of the resurrection narratives, Fr Martelet soon shows that he is not going to be ensnared in the quasi-physical understanding of the risen body which so many orthodox theologians have embraced. He is determined that the relationship between the risen Lord and the faithful should be expressed in terms of Spirit.[97] The risen body must be regarded as a relation and not as a thing,[98] and he says with great boldness that if you insist that the body is spatially in heaven you cannot have it in the eucharist 'really'. It must be 'symbolically'. He thereby differentiates himself alike from Thomas Aquinas and the Reformers.[99] He expresses the problem with admirable lucidity: 'It is the Resurrection that obliges us to call *identical*, and yet different, the body which is born of the Virgin, which suffers, which dies on the cross, which rises again in glory, and which is given to us in the eucharistic meal.'[100] It is quite true that the word 'body' is applied in the New Testament to all these various entities, and therefore they must have something in common – Jesus Christ no doubt! Martelet solves the problem by regarding the last two of these (the body which rises in glory and the body which is given in the eucharist) as a relation. I think this is a very hopeful approach, one which obviates all sorts of difficulties into which the traditional account of the risen body has run. But I think that nothing but a strong regard for the need to preserve traditional language can justify the use of the word '*identical*' to cover all these meanings.

The difficulty of using 'identity' language is highlighted by a passage from George Tyrrell, quoted by Darwell Stone: 'When we are told that Christ's sacramental body is not referred to space *ratione sui*, but only *ratione accidentis*; that it is not moved when the species are carried in procession; that we are not nearer to it at the altar than at the North Pole; we can only say that this *ratione sui* consideration does not concern us, nor is it any part of God's revelation.'[101] Tyrrell is referring to attempts to refine the doctrine of transubstantiation, and to protect it from crude misunderstanding. The body of Christ in the eucharist is defined as having no relation to space as far as concerns itself, but only as far as concerns its accidents. Tyrrell's protest well underlines the truth that the attempt of the philosopher or theologian to make sense of a doctrine of 'literal' identification between the physical body of the historical Jesus and the consecrated species only ends by doing away with the very point that identification is supposed to conserve. Whatever the consecrated species is, even according to Thomistic doctrine, it is not the physical body of Christ.

Martelet remarks very wisely: 'We should not look on the Holy Spirit as a substitute for the glorified Christ in the latter's alleged incapabilities in relation to space.'[102] No, certainly not a 'substitute', and if he is brought in as a substitute the result will be merely confusing. But if from the resurrection onwards we regard the entire relationship between Christ and the Word, and between the Word revealed in Christ and Christians, in terms of Spirit, we shall find that a great many intellectual difficulties are avoided. This, I believe, Martelet in effect does, and this is why his book is so valuable. We shall return to it in a later chapter and find it no less valuable there.

I must now take issue with a very distinguished New Testament scholar from Cambridge, who, in a recent book, has dealt with some of the questions we are concerned with here. C. F. D. Moule in *The Origin of Christology*[103] has no doubt that Paul, the author of Hebrews, and the author of the Fourth Gospel all hold a doctrine of pre-existence. He raises the question of the mode of pre-existence which these respective writers had in mind. Of Hebrews he writes: 'But we are still left asking how the individual of the ministry and the post-resurrection glory is related to that pre-existent Being' (referred to in Heb. 1.1–4).[104] In the ensuing pages he goes on to claim that both Paul and John hold that Jesus was an individual, regard him as divine, and have a doctrine of pre-existence. Then he writes: 'It is not easy to conceive of a genuinely human person being conscious of his own pre-existence and it would not be right to build upon John 17.5 as though this in itself constituted evidence of Jesus' *ipsissima vox*. But it is arguable that when Paul (Col. 1.15f.) and John articulate the belief in the preexistence of Christ, they are only drawing out the implications of their experience of him as transcending the temporal.'[105] And he goes on to argue that it is not enough to say that the Logos was pre-existent and that 'when Jesus came he fitted perfectly with God's design and thus coincided (as it were) with the pre-existent Logos. This is rationally intelligible and attractive, and it leaves room for Jesus himself to be a product of biological evolution. But then what becomes of the sequel?'[106] And he goes on to maintain in effect that since the New Testament writers and subsequent Christian experience require a Christ who is both an individual and one capable of divine functions in being omnipresent and communicable to all, we must posit the same sort of being before the incarnation.

Since it is the central issue of this work and since I believe that this very eminent scholar is mistaken in some of the conclusions he draws about the New Testament witness, it might be best if I set out my reply to this important argument of Moule's in numbered paragraphs:

1. A form of Logos doctrine is perfectly comprehensible and does not in itself create any particular difficulties in the light of modern thought. This is the doctrine that in God we can distinguish three modes of being. The second of these, the mode wherein he is orientated towards his creation in general and man in particular, we can denote God the Word or Logos. This is the sort of Logos doctrine put forward by Tillich and Pittenger, and accepted by me in *Grace and Truth*. There is no intrinsic difficulty in comprehending how the Logos in this sense could indwell Jesus *kat'eudokian*. According to this doctrine pre-existence would mean simply the fact that God was Three in One, and that one of the Three was the Logos. This doctrine could be elaborated by saying that in fact humanity is the supreme form in which God the Word can be revealed. I defended such an extension of the Logos doctrine in *Grace and Truth*. Certainly this doctrine does raise acutely the question posed by Moule: 'But then what becomes of the sequel?' It is the main aim of this work to try to answer this question. But Moule requires something more than this: he requires a personal divine being, Jesus Christ, existing from eternity and perhaps conscious of so existing throughout the period of his incarnation. Indeed, his requirement reminds us very much of Barth's difficult doctrine that in some sense Jesus *as man* was pre-existent. Moule makes this a necessity of his christology because he wishes to preserve a personal continuity for the incarnate One from the pre-existent period,

through the period of historical incarnation, into the period of post-incarnation risen glory. I would prefer to leave the discussion of the New Testament evidence for this view till Chapter 4 where it will get full consideration. But I must state at this point that the necessary *historical* evidence for this view is simply not adequate for the purpose. The three synoptic gospels give us no hint of a Jesus conscious of existence in a pre-incarnate state. We must, if we are honest, conclude that John's attribution of such consciousness to Jesus is a construction of the evangelist or his school. I would also add that philosophically it is extremely difficult to defend an incarnation conceived on these lines, and that, when we pass to the post-resurrection period and find an individual humanity called Jesus available by prayer and sacrament to all faithful Christians, it becomes impossible to defend. I would refer to Keith Ward's article 'Incarnation or Inspiration – A False Dichotomy' which I discuss in a later chapter.

2. Moule suggests that 'when Paul (Col. 1.15ff.) and John articulate the belief in the pre-existence of Christ, they are only drawing out the implications of their experience of him as transcending the temporal'. Presumably Moule means 'their experience as Christians in the post-Easter community'. He can hardly mean that they had personal experience of the historical Jesus, or that they relied on eyewitnesses who had. In other words, he believes that they argued from 'post-existence' to 'pre-existence'. I think the situation was a great deal more complicated than that, as I hope to show in the next chapter. In any case we today can hardly argue like that. We must conclude that, whatever Paul and the author of Hebrews believed about the pre-existent being whom, on occasion, they could refer to as Jesus Christ, John was not justified on historical grounds in attributing to Jesus knowledge of a pre-incarnate existence. We must therefore seek some other method of presenting our doctrine of incarnation.

3. I do not think Moule is right in his conclusion that Paul and the author of Hebrews at least attributed pre-existence to Jesus because in their experience he 'transcends the temporal'. They needed a doctrine of pre-existence not primarily in order to relegate Jesus to the eternal supra-temporal realm, but because they wanted to trace his activity in history in Israel's history. In other words, the primary impulse behind the pre-existence doctrine was not religious experience but salvation history. They realized that they could not claim that Jesus fulfilled the

scriptures unless they could show that God's revelation of himself to Israel of old was in some sense through Jesus Christ. Hence the primary need for a theory of pre-existence. I do not deny that their experience of God in Christ in the Spirit made it easier for them to accept this conclusion, but I do not think it was the primary motive.

4. When we go beyond the authentic Paul and Hebrews, and consider Colossians and the Fourth Gospel, we have a somewhat different situation.[107] By the time these documents came to be written (after AD 70, I believe), educated and thoughtful Christians had to face the question: 'Do you Christians believe in two gods?' There is some evidence that the community in which the Fourth Gospel was written was being taxed with this question by the Jews. And the author of the Pastorals (which I date about AD 100–105), virtually does believe in two gods. At least he uses the title *sotēr* indiscriminately for God and Jesus, and in one place, I believe (Titus 2.13), actually uses the word *theos* of Jesus. A very short time after the Pastorals were written Ignatius of Antioch is using *theos* (always modified with a pronoun or adjectival phrase) quite freely of Jesus. This posed a problem to Christian theologians the only solution to which was to conclude that we must admit the existence of distinctions within the godhead. Hence something like a Logos doctrine. Moule himself in his admirable introduction to the New Testament has characterized Col. 1.15–19 as 'a Logos doctrine in all but the actual term'.[108] But by this time of course the concept of an individual divine being active in Israel's history also formed part of their christological tradition. Both features, Logos doctrine and a pre-existent being active in Israel's history, are found in the Fourth Gospel.

5. What about 'the sequel'? What did Paul, the author of Hebrews, and John believe about the nature of the risen Christ and his relation to Christians? We do not know how the author of Hebrews would have answered this question. Moule does not believe that he had a corporate conception of the risen Christ as Paul and John had.[109] We do not have much clue as to how John would have related the risen Jesus to him whom he represented as saying 'I am the vine; you are the branches', but he does not present us with a doctrine of the body of Christ related to the church, as Paul does. Paul's doctrine of the body of Christ was instigated by a desire to work out an account of how Christians are related to God in Christ, and why it is that though

Christ is now risen, we are not. His doctrine is firmly orientated towards the parousia and its obscurity is occasioned not least by the fact that Paul is most anxious to speak in terms of spirit rather than of flesh. I think we can reasonably enough equate Paul's 'spiritual body' with our modern concept of 'personality'. We must therefore conclude, if we are to retain an equivalent to Paul's doctrine of the body of Christ, that Christians are now by faith related somehow to the personality of Jesus, and will be more intimately related hereafter. I believe I can include all this in my account of the risen Christ without incurring the difficulties concerning the limitations of humanity and the spatial quality of a body which traditional christology has encountered.

This discussion of Moule's christology has brought us to the very verge of the topic which occupies the next chapter. But first we should take a glance at what the Eastern Orthodox tradition has to contribute to a solution of this problem.

I take my text from Vladimir Lossky's well known work *The Mystical Theology of the Eastern Church*.[110] He writes as follows:

> At the moment of the incarnation, the divine light was concentrated, so to speak in Christ, the God-man, 'in whom dwelleth the whole fullness of the godhead bodily'. That is to say that the humanity of Christ was deified by hypostatic union with the divine nature; that Christ during his earthly life always shed forth the divine light – which, however, remained invisible to most men. The Transfiguration was not a phenomenon circumscribed in time and space; Christ underwent no change at that moment even in his human nature, but a change occurred in the awareness of the apostles, who for a time received the power to see their Master as he was, resplendent in the eternal light of his godhead.

Lossky then writes about the experience which the saints can enjoy even in this life, suggesting by his language that God's communication of himself to us in Christ so transcends the bounds of what we know of humanity that the problems we have been concerned with simply disappear.[111]

Now, certainly, anyone taking this view of Christ's nature has no reason to experience any difficulty in expressing how the risen and ascended Word is related to the humanity which he assumed, or to the faithful. Christ has his humanity so completely under control, so to speak, that it need form no barrier between him and God or him and Christians. There need not even be any question of a risen body endowed with ubiquity because a humanity that was deified from the first moment of the conception of Jesus in Mary's womb need not be subject to any physical limitations whatever. Even during the period of the incarnation it is difficult to see how any limit need be put to what it could do. If Jesus as he appeared during the time of the Transfiguration is the *real* incarnate Word, then Jesus as he appeared apart from the Transfiguration is something less than real and at best an example of God incognito. The way in which Krishna is described in the Bhagavad Gita provides a most striking parallel. Krishna does at first appear in the guise of Arjuna's charioteer, but this assumed character is fairly thin and is penetrated easily by Arjuna. When at Arjuna's request, he brings about his *pratyaksata*, his manifestation of himself in his true being, we realize that his appearance as a man was a temporary phenomenon only.

But this immunity of the Eastern Orthodox tradition from the difficulties into which we Westerners have run is purchased at a heavy price, one which most of us would be quite unwilling to pay. In effect they so modify the incarnation of the Word that they make it look much more like a theophany than an incarnation. They have taken one side of the two-sided Formula of Chalcedon and so emphasized it that the other side is in danger of disappearing altogether. This is no doubt primarily because for historical reasons the Eastern church had to pay much more attention to the Monophysite tradition than the West had to do. But it is also because the Eastern Orthodox theologians have so far made no serious attempt to come to terms with biblical criticism.

If we consider their account of the incarnate Word from the point of view of what we know about the development of christology in the earliest community, we must conclude that they put far too much reliance on the historical accuracy of the account of Jesus given in the Fourth Gospel. It is from there primarily that the concept of the 'divinization' or 'deification' of the human nature of the Word comes. There are signs, it is true, of a growing tendency to 'divinize' the historical Jesus if one begins from Mark and then reads Matthew and Luke, but the Fourth Gospel represents a big leap forward in this respect. And certainly the only proper historical conclusion is that the earlier the sources of the records about Jesus, the fewer are the signs of this 'divinization'.

It may indeed be pointed out that in the passage quoted from Lossky it is the Transfiguration that is taken as the criterion for the true being of the Incarnate Word, and the Transfiguration is not mentioned in the Fourth Gospel. On the contrary, it occurs in what is probably the earliest written record of Jesus, Mark's gospel. Here perhaps is the point where the Easterners would be most outraged, for Western scholars would have to reply that the narrative of the Transfiguration is not one which can be regarded as possessing a high historical value. It may rather be classed as a cult-story. Though there are probably historical events behind it, we cannot recover them with confidence, and least of all can we regard the description of Jesus' appearance during the Transfiguration event as a sure criterion for his actual historical being. Above all, to treat the Transfiguration narrative as the norm by which we judge the historical reliability of the other narratives about Jesus in the synoptic gospels would be to go against all the canons of historical evidence. No doubt by taking this stance we would lay ourselves open to the accusation on the part of the Easterners that we have capitulated to the rationalism of the *Aufklärung*. We can only reply that we are not willing to base our belief in Christ on legendary material. We must be able to distinguish the historical Jesus from the legendary Krishna. The concept of the divinization of the humanity of the Incarnate Word leads inevitably towards Docetism and legend. Whatever modifications we may have to make to traditional dogma, our first duty is to the historical truth as far as we can recover it.

Let us try to draw some preliminary conclusions from our study of the traditional doctrine of the risen Christ, beginning with some remarks about the resurrection narratives and then setting out the conclusions.

I took the view in *Grace and Truth* that the resurrection of Jesus was a real event and that the tomb was empty. I believe he was raised from the dead by the power of God and did so appear to his disciples as to convince them that he had risen and was alive with God in the dimension of Spirit. I have not withdrawn from this position in any way. But this belief is quite compatible with the realization that the narratives of the resurrection in the gospels are fragmentary, unharmonized, and to some extent contain legendary elements. In particular we are not justified in drawing any hard historical conclusions as to the precise nature of the 'body' of the risen Lord. He was recognizable, with difficulty it seems, as he had to be if the appearance were to have any effect. As to his capacity to eat, to pass through closed doors, to be touched etc.; we do not know and should not try to draw any positive conclusions. His actual physical corpse, the body crucified and buried, disappeared. Its fate does not concern us, any more than a believing Christian should be concerned about the fate of his own body at death. We may believe that God disposed of the corpse of Jesus as he, and only he, had the power to do. It also follows that we must not put any emphasis on the historical character of the ascension: it is only narrated by Luke, and it seems that he had theological reasons for including it in his scheme of things. Matthew gives us a parting scene but no ascension. John does seem to know of an ascension (John 20.17) but does not describe it. The relation of the twenty-first chapter of the Fourth Gospel to the rest of the work is a notorious problem. In it the last words of Jesus to his disciples are 'Follow me'. There is no mention of an ascension afterwards. Still less of course can we insist on an exact period of forty days between the resurrection and the ascension. These considerations in themselves must considerably influence our doctrine of the nature of the risen Christ. Westcott, Benson, Swete and Tait all accepted without question the historicity of the forty days and the ascension.

I conclude from this study of the traditional doctrine that we ought not to claim that as a result of the incarnation humanity is more closely associated with the godhead or that Christians have access to God by means of Jesus' risen humanity. Still less do I believe that we ought to be concerned to link the risen body of Jesus in some way either to the church or to the eucharist. This last statement will have to be explained in later chapters: I am very far from repudiating either a link between Jesus and Christians after death or a doctrine of the presence of God the Word in the eucharist. But I believe that only confusion can result from the attempt to construct some ontological link between the body of the historical Jesus and the church or the eucharist. My reasons for these far-reaching conclusions are as follows:

(a) The concept of a 'glorified humanity' sitting on the throne of the universe or at God's right hand is meaningless. Humanity, if it means anything means finiteness. That which is finite cannot be God: it can be used to manifest God but it cannot be identical with God. Still less can Christ's humanity be available to all the faithful in prayer and religious experience. This availability is the function of God not man. We have seen that this last conclusion was very widely accepted by the Western tradition: it can enlist the support of Augustine, Thomas Aquinas, and the Reformed tradition stemming from Calvin.

(b) It satisfies the New Testament witness and the experience of the church if we are content to say that as a result of the incarnation all men can now have access to God the Word known in the image of Jesus Christ. I must refer to the ensuing chapters to explain what I mean by this last phrase. God is now known in the fullness of his self-revelation in the form or image of Jesus Christ, and is available in the sacraments as such.

(c) The doctrine of the glorified humanity seems to suggest that some of the greatest figures of the Old Testament revelation, such as Hosea, Jeremiah, or the Servant of the Lord portrayed in Deutero-Isaiah, not to mention the anonymous authors of so many psalms of intimate communion with God, could not have come really close to God because they could not partake in the glorified humanity of the Word. But this is contrary to the evidence: what they lacked was scope of knowledge of God, not intimacy of communion. We might also add that many people in other religious traditions appear to have got very close to God, and I certainly would not want to deny the validity of their religious experience.

(d) At first sight these conclusions might seem to empty the incarnation of its distinctive significance. Does it not become merely a temporary incident in God's dealings with men? No, because the revelation of God's character was only fully and adequately made known in Jesus Christ. Most especially do we find in the cross the very manifestation of his nature. Only in Jesus Christ is this revelation disclosed and only in the community of the church is a satisfactory relation with God the Word permanently and continuously available. Moreover the revelation in Jesus Christ mediates a universal revelation. Virtually none of the figures of the Old Testament looked beyond Israel. Even today Judaism can hardly be described as a universal religion. All this is summed up in the doctrine of God as Trinity, which I believe must follow from the nature of the revelation in Jesus Christ.

(e) I do not wish to exclude the risen Jesus from a continuing part in God's economy of salvation. He lives, king of saints, in the company of the blessed in heaven. We do not know what our relation to him will be hereafter because we do not know the conditions under which we may hope to exist then. Perhaps Paul's claim that we, with him, will then enjoy a 'spiritual body' is as good a symbol for that future state as any. We do, of course, hope 'to see him as he is'. But our relation now on earth is with God the Word known to us in the image of Jesus Christ. We must now proceed to a more detailed explanation of what that means.

Three

Paul and Pre-existence

In Chapter 4 I intend to make use of what I believe to be the Pauline doctrine of the pre-existence of the Son of God as an analogy for the particular view of the relation of the risen Christ to believers which I wish to expound. But recently the whole question of this alleged doctrine of pre-existence has been raised in an acute form in a valuable and learned work by Dr J. D. G. Dunn called *Christology in the Making*.[1] Dunn maintains that Paul has no doctrine of a pre-existent being, whether called Christ or the Son, at all; that the doctrine is only lightly sketched in Hebrews, and that it appears for the first time in an explicit and deliberate form in the Fourth Gospel. Moreover he seems to accept Colossians as being Pauline, so his denial of a pre-existence doctrine is extended to that epistle also. If Dunn is right, I cannot use Paul's doctrine of pre-existence as an analogy for my approach to the question of the status of the risen Christ, for Paul had no such idea. So, before I can be justified in writing of a Pauline analogy, I must devote a chapter to an attempt to show that Dunn is too sweeping in his elimination of a doctrine of pre-existence from Paul's writings. I find that the subject falls into three main sections:

(a) 'God sent his Son . . .'

We begin by considering two Pauline passages which on the face of it would seem to imply that God's Son was sent from heaven, and thereby to posit some sort of pre-existence for the Son. The first is Galatians 4.4:

But when the time had fully come, God sent forth his Son, born of woman, born under the law . . .

The word for 'sent forth' here is *exapesteilen*, which Dunn notes can be used in the LXX for the sending of a heavenly messenger, or for the sending of a prophet.[2] He does, however, point to a remarkable parallel in Wisdom 9.10, where the author in the person of Solomon prays (my translation):

Send (Wisdom) from the holy heavens and despatch her from thy throne of glory.

The first 'send' is *exaposteilon* and 'despatch' is *pempson*, precisely the two verbs used in the two respective passages we are dealing with. He thinks the parallel is modified by the fact that Wisdom is feminine, and therefore could not readily suggest to Paul the thought of God sending his Son; but he himself refers to two passages in Philo where precisely this difficulty is dealt with. In *De Fuga et Inventione* 51.[3] Philo wishes to represent Wisdom as a father, and he writes: 'How, pray, can Wisdom, the daughter of God, be rightly spoken of as a father? Is it because, while Wisdom's name is feminine, her nature is manly? As indeed all the virtues have women's titles, but powers and activities of consummate man.' And he goes on to say that the reason why Wisdom is given a feminine gender is because it comes after God, and is therefore inferior to God. In the second passage, *De Abrahamo* (100–2), he argues that genders are often misleadingly attached to nouns, and we must not be deceived by them. Dunn suggests that this sort of speculation is peculiar to Philo because of the complexity of his allegorizing;[4] but it seems to me that Philo is making a perfectly reasonable point: the gender of an abstract noun at least gives no clue as to its real meaning. Hence I think it is reasonable to regard Wisdom 9.10 as a significant parallel and to infer that the fact that Wisdom is feminine in Greek and Hebrew would not necessarily have inhibited Paul from seeing in this Wisdom passage a hint of the pre-existence of the Son.

The second passage runs thus:

For God has done what the law . . . could not do, sending his Son in the likeness of sinful flesh and for sin, he condemned sin in the flesh (Romans 8.3).

Dunn sees the force of the objection: 'why emphasize "born of woman" if there was not also the implication of heavenly birth?' and of course the same objection applies to the phrase 'in the likeness of sinful flesh'. He replies that these phrases are meant to indicate that Jesus partook of our own sinful condition. He adds that the chief intention is soteriological rather than christological.[5] Of the Romans passage he writes that it refers simply to the sending of a man, not a heavenly being. The salvation was accomplished on the cross. It is, in fact, Adam christology: 'the one who is God's son (prior to his death as well as after his resurrection) is one whose divine commissioning did not lift him above human sin and suffering, but rather brought him condemnation of sin in the flesh through his death as a man of "sinful flesh" and as "a sacrifice for sin".'[6] He later adds: 'Paul thought of Jesus' sonship in terms of his death.'[7]

It seems to me that this argument of Dunn's is something like special pleading. If Paul had only meant that the man Jesus Christ was sinless, he could have said so straightforwardly; there would have been no need for him to say that Jesus was 'born of woman'. Suppose he was talking of a prophet, about whom there was no question of pre-existence, we would certainly not expect any reference to 'born of a woman' or 'in the likeness of sinful flesh'. Indeed Dunn himself in another context offers an excellent example: he refers to Jeremiah 49.14 (LXX 30.8); Obadiah 1: 'a messenger has been sent out among the nations'. No one, Dunn claims, would infer that the messenger was a pre-existent being.[8] Precisely; and there is no phrase here about the messenger being born of a woman or being sent in the likeness of sinful flesh. When such phrases are used they must imply something extra, and that something can only be some form of pre-existence.

We may point to two more pieces of evidence in favour of the view that Paul does have pre-existence in mind. In Gal. 4.6, two verses after the reference to God having sent his Son, Paul writes of God having sent the Spirit of his Son into our hearts (using the same verb *exapesteilen*). This sending was certainly from God, or from heaven. The other piece of evidence occurs in Romans 8.32:

He (God) did not spare his own Son, but gave him up for us all.

Dunn interprets this as meaning that Jesus, who was God's Son in some obscure sense before his death, became God's Son (or was declared God's Son) in his death. God certainly cannot be described as 'giving up' his Son to death if Jesus only became God's Son at his death. In any case, on Dunn's hypothesis the actual 'giving up' consisted not in any action on God's part but on Jesus' decision to accept death. It seems a strange way of describing it. Once again, we find that the conclusion that Paul did hold a doctrine of pre-existence is by far the simplest explanation of the evidence.

(b) 'being in the form of God'

Dunn now deals with three further Pauline passages in which scholars have detected a doctrine of pre-existence, and argues that such a conclusion is unnecessary in each case. The first is I Corinthians 15.45–47:

> Thus it is written, 'The first man Adam became a living being; the last Adam became a life-giving spirit'. But it is not the spiritual which is first but the physical, and then the spiritual. The first man was from the earth, a man of dust; the second man is from heaven.

Dunn claims that this passage is quite opposed to the concept of pre-existence: 'When Paul uses Adam language explicitly he is referring primarily to Christ risen and exalted'.[9] 'To interpret "the man from heaven" as a reference to pre-existence mistakes the eschatological character of Christ's Adam-ness. Paul explicitly *denies* that Christ precedes Adam: "the spiritual (= heavenly) is not first, but the physical (= earthly), then the spiritual" (v. 46)'.[10] 'As the first Adam came into existence (*egeneto*) at creation the beginning of the old age, so the last Adam (as such) came into existence at the resurrection, the beginning of the age to come'. 'It was by playing the rôle of Adam that Christ became last Adam'. 'Christ's death was his act of righteousness, his act of obedience. . . . But beyond death he re-emerged as a new Adam'.[11]

There is a certain obscurity here as to when, according to Dunn, Christ actually became the last Adam, very like the obscurity we noted in the last section as to when Christ became Son. Dunn would like to be able to postpone the appearance of the Second Adam until the resurrection, but of course he cannot afford to do this because it is the act of obedience of the Second Adam that is all-important, and that must be located in the death (better still, in the entire life and death) of Jesus. Dunn therefore seems to envisage a scheme according

to which Christ reverses the career of the old Adam with some exact-
ness: the old Adam began very glorious, disobeyed and ended as a
slave (of sin, or of the elemental powers). The Second Adam began
as a slave (of the Law, perhaps of the powers), obeyed God even to
death and ended up a new glorious Adam, spiritual and heavenly.
Moreover, believers, by partaking (sacramentally, mystically) in this
death, become part of the new humanity.

The difficulty with this interpretation is two-fold: how can the
Second Adam be described as 'the man of heaven' (*ho epouranios*, v. 48)
and as being 'from heaven' (*ex ouranou*, v. 47) if he only acquired these
characteristics at the resurrection? In order to carry out his act of
salvation he needed to be the heavenly man at least during the time of
his life on earth. Dunn seems to give us the picture of a Jesus who
began by being a member of the first Adam, but became the Second
Adam at the resurrection. But this will not meet the soteriological
purpose it is designed to serve. Dunn seem to be aware of this, for he
suggests at one point that in Paul's view Jesus had lived during his
life on earth 'according to the Spirit'.[12] This is hardly consistent with
Dunn's insistence that only at the resurrection did the spiritual Adam
come into existence.

The second objection is of a more philosophical nature. We can
imagine a doctrine of Christ that saw him in the rôle of a prophet as a
representative of mankind, perhaps designated as such by God. But
this is not adequate to meet the demand which Dunn (or, for that
matter, Paul himself) makes on the risen Christ: he must be parallel
to the old Adam in the sense of being a corporate personality. All
believers are to die and rise with him in his death and resurrection.
How could anyone imagine that a single human individual, no matter
how obedient to God, could fill this rôle? We must have a figure that
can be a corporate personality. But that is precisely what Philo's
ouranios anthrōpos is.[13] Dunn does consider the relevance for our study
of Philo's references to 'the heavenly man', but he dismisses this concept as a 'bloodless idea'.[14] Here, I believe, he is being less than just
to Philo. Once grant the possibility that there could be a concept of a
pre-existent ideal man, then it is quite beside the mark to dismiss it as
'bloodless'. Dunn objects to Philo's two epithets which he applies to
this heavenly man, *noētos* and *asōmatos*. But it is difficult to see how a
pre-existent heavenly being could be anything but 'apprehended by

thought' and 'non-material'. The same epithets could be applied to God, but no one would think of dismissing the idea of God as 'bloodless'.

It seems more in accordance with the evidence to conclude that when Paul describes the Second Adam as *epouranios* and *ex ouranou* ('heavenly' and 'from heaven'), he meant that Christ had always been thus. Christians also are to become *epouranioi* (v. 48), but as bearing the image of *ho epouranios* in the same way as Adam originally bore the image of God. If Dunn's interpretation were correct, Paul would more accurately have written that the Second Adam was *eis ouranon* 'directed to heaven'. He says *ex ouranou*, 'from heaven', in direct contrast to the old Adam who was *ek gēs*, 'of the earth'. This phrase refers to the origin of Adam or to the material of which he was made. So the Second Adam had his origin in heaven. He was after the first Adam in the order of appearance on earth, not in the order of being.

We now turn to the other two passages on which Dunn relies in order to prove his case, Philippians 2.6–11 and II Corinthians 8.9. They run as follows:

[Christ Jesus], who, though he was in the form of God (*en morphē/i theou huparchōn*) did not count equality with God a thing to be grasped, but emptied himself, taking the form of a servant, being born in the likeness of men (*en homoiōmati anthrōpōn genomenos*)

For you know the grace of our Lord Jesus Christ, that though he was rich, yet for your sake he became poor, so that by his poverty you might become rich.

Dunn is determined to interpret the passage from Philippians 2 in terms which do not imply pre-existence. He therefore takes *en morphē/i theou huparchōn* as meaning that Christ, like Adam, was in the image of God, not that he was in the form of God. This implies understanding *to einai isa theō/i* ('equality with God') in the sense of 'bearing God's image', not a very likely conclusion. Dunn writes: 'If Christ walks in Adam's footsteps, then Christ need be no more pre-existent than Adam'. Again 'Whether the choice was made by the pre-existent Christ or the historical Jesus is immaterial'; and he suggests that Jesus' whole life was a choice.[15]

The difficulty with this explanation (apart from the unsatisfactory account of what 'equality with God' means) is that it does not seem to make room for all the elements involved in the passage in question. We have to have a period during which Christ was 'in the form of God', then a choice by Christ as a result of which he 'emptied himself' and became a servant. The parallel with Adam which Dunn attempts to draw is fallacious, for in the case of Adam there was first a period of innocence, then a fall resulting in his becoming a slave. There is nothing in Jesus' life corresponding to Adam's choice: Adam chose to disobey God. Jesus chose to obey and thus became a slave. When did this happen? To say that it makes no difference whether the choice was made by the pre-existent or the historical Jesus is simply to ignore the real issue. In any case, there must be some contrast between being in the form of God and being a servant. According to Dunn's account there was no contrast at all: the man Jesus, who was, like all men, in the image of God, also became a slave. That is a totally inadequate explanation of what Paul means.

Dunn's explanation becomes even more unsatisfactory when he comes to deal with II Cor. 8.9. He writes: 'a reference to Jesus' own material poverty freely embraced cannot be dismissed out of hand'.[16] This might make sense if there was any evidence that Jesus had ever been materially rich. If like St Francis he had given up riches to embrace the life of an itinerant preacher, this explanation might hold. But there is of course no evidence whatever of this. In the same passage therefore Dunn advances another explanation: 'the richness of his communion with God . . . set in sharp contrast with his desolation on the cross'. Here is free speculation indeed! We are often warned by New Testament scholars not to attempt to go too far in attempting to reconstruct the religious experience of Jesus on the basis of the gospels, which do at least give us some sort of account of his life. But here is Dunn suggesting that Paul in this phrase is referring to an important element in the religious experience of the historical Jesus, Paul who betrays the absolute minimum knowledge of, or interest in, the life of the historical Jesus before the passion! The improbability of his speculation is a measure of the improbability of Dunn's explanation of this phrase. When, finally, he describes Jesus as 'one who freely embraced the lot of the fallen Adam', we have to remind ourselves that he does not refer to Jesus' pre-existence, though I must confess that without the presupposition of pre-existence the phrase seems to me devoid of significance. If it was a free choice, he must have been able not to make it. On the supposition that Jesus was in Paul's view simply a human individual, he had no choice about it.

(c) *'that rock was Christ'*

We must now consider a third source of evidence that Paul held a doctrine of pre-existence. This is the claim that Paul sometimes traces the activity of the pre-existent Christ in Israel's history. Here we are in a somewhat different position for Dunn flatly denies that any such evidence exists. Indeed he goes further than that, and makes the very far-reaching claim that no Christian writer makes any such suggestion before Justin! He writes: 'We may doubt whether any Jewish Christian would have been tempted to anticipate Justin by seeing in any of these [sc. theophanies or angelophanies in the OT] Christ in a pre-existent form'.[17] And later: 'There is no evidence that any Christian writer thought of Jesus as actually present in Israel's past, either as the angel of the Lord or as "the Lord" himself.'[18] This is an astonishing statement. Quite apart from the question of whether such a phenomenon occurs in Paul's writings, one would have thought that Dunn would have given some attention to the Fourth Gospel before committing himself to so absolute a negative. Let us therefore begin by looking at the evidence for this belief in the New Testament outside Paul's writings, and then work our way backwards in time towards Paul.

We begin with Jude 5. I take the Epistle of Jude to be one of the later books in the New Testament, but if it is earlier, the argument is of course stronger. The text in the RSV runs thus:

> Now I desire to remind you, though you were once for all fully informed that he who saved a people out of the land of Egypt, afterwards destroyed those who did not believe.

But this translation does not correspond to any known version of the Greek text. It is, in fact, based on a conjectural restoration of the text by Westcott and Hort in their edition of the Greek New Testament. The most likely reading is that adopted in the Bible Societies' version of the Greek New Testament.[19] 'Jesus, who saved a people out of the land of Egypt, afterwards destroyed. . . .' This is read by Codex Alexandrinus and Vaticanus, by two other Greek unicals, by various manuscripts of the Old Latin, by the Ethiopic, and by two early Fathers. A modified version of this, 'God Christ saved a people' is read by papyrus 72; and another modification, which still includes the name 'Jesus', by at least three other Greek uncials, by another manuscript of the Old Latin, and by two versions of the Coptic. The next best attested reading, *kurios* or *ho kurios* ('Lord' or 'the Lord') is supported by some of the Fathers, and also by Sinaiticus and many other Greek uncials. The third variant, 'God' (*ho theos*) is poorly attested. Even if one opts for '*ho kurios*' one is still adopting a reading that implies the activity of the pre-existent Christ. According to the normal criteria of textual criticism, therefore, we must conclude that it is very likely that the doctrine of the pre-existent Christ's activity in Israel's history occurs in Jude. No doubt the author identified the pre-existent Christ with the angel in the pillar of cloud, a point that has some bearing on our discussion of I Cor. 10.1–4 later on.

Next we turn to the Fourth Gospel. We could point to several places where the doctrine of the pre-existent Christ active in Israel's history could be detected with much probability, but we will confine ourselves to one passage where it seems to be quite undeniable. The author quotes Isaiah 6.10, and then writes:

Isaiah said this because he saw his glory and spoke of him.

The words 'his glory' and 'him' must refer to Jesus Christ. In the context it could not possibly indicate God the Father.[20] John has identified the Lord of hosts whom Isaiah saw in his vision in the temple, with the pre-existent Christ (John 12.4).

Here, then are two clear examples of this doctrine in the pages of the New Testament. Neither of them can be subsumed under the various categories by means of which Dunn hopes to dispose of all alleged examples of Christ's pre-existent activity, to wit: 'prophecies which could be taken to apply to their own day, or types which could now be seen to foreshadow the reality of Christ, or occasionally allegories which could be interpreted christologically'.[21] We now turn to the Epistle to the Hebrews for further evidence. Dunn admits a sort of pre-existence doctrine in Hebrews, but emphasizes that it is only an 'ideal', 'Platonic' sort of pre-existence. We have already considered this and concluded that this sort of epithet is beside the point if it is used as a means of explaining away pre-existence doctrine. But Dunn goes on to deny that the evidence in Hebrews supports 'a real personal pre-existence'.[22] I believe we can point to evidence that this is exactly what the author of Hebrews believed. I will confine myself to two points. The first concerns Heb. 11.23–27. The peculiarity of this passage is that Moses is described in verse 26 thus:

> He considered abuse suffered for the Christ greater wealth than the treasures of Egypt.

The RSV translation is not literal here. The Greek phrase is *ton oneidismon tou Christou* 'the reproach of Christ' or 'of the Messiah'. How can Moses, who lived hundreds of years before the birth of Christ, have suffered 'the reproach of Christ'? Most editors explain it as a brief way of saying that the reproach of God's chosen people was the reproach of Christ; or that Israel was an anointed people. Among such is Dunn. He, very appropriately, refers to Psalm 89.50–51 (LXX 88.51–52). He quotes the LXX text, which refers to *ton oneidismon tōn doulōn sou* ('the reproach of thy servants') and *ōneidisan to antallagma tou christou sou*, which he renders: 'how your enemies abused the succession of your anointed one'. He explains it thus: 'the thought is of the sufferings of the elect people (and subsequently king) as a typological prefigurement of Christ's sufferings'.[23] Now we must suppose that the author of Hebrews read his Bible in Greek. It is most unlikely that he would (or could) consult the Hebrew. He certainly does have Psalm 89.50–51 in mind here. But the LXX would not suggest a kingly succession to him. Dunn is mistaken in rendering *to antallagma* here with 'the succession'. The word never bears that meaning, in the LXX or anywhere else. Its normal meaning is 'price paid', or 'substitute offered'. Liddell and Scott[24] give the meaning as 'that which is given or taken in exchange'. So that phrase *to antallagma tou christou* would mean to the author of Hebrews 'the substitution of the Christ'. It is very likely indeed that he saw in this phrase a reference to Christ's vicarious suffering, which he finds pre-enacted in the exodus from Egypt.[25]

But we can be more specific than this: when the author of Hebrews describes Moses as preferring the reproach of the Messiah to the riches of Egypt, he must be referring to the period when Moses had fled from Egypt after killing the Egyptian and then returned to take up the cause of his people after the experience of the burning bush: 'By faith he left Egypt not being afraid of the anger of the king' must refer to this flight and not to the Exodus itself, because in between this incident and the crossing of the Red Sea narrated in verse 29 comes the mention of the Passover in verse 28.[26] What lies between verses 27 and 28, therefore, is probably the incident of the burning bush. Indeed this is in all likelihood referred to in the phrase in verse 27: 'for he endured as seeing him who is invisible'. The Invisible had made himself visible in the burning bush. This is confirmed by the words which the angel in the bush utters in the name of God in Exodus 3.7: 'I have seen the oppression (*kakōsin*) of my people. . . . I have come down to rescue them.' These words are actually echoed in Heb. 11.25: 'choosing rather to share ill-treatment with the people of God (*sunkakoucheisthai*)'. The pre-existent Christ had promised that he would come down and rescue his people from oppression, and Moses decides to share the oppression that Christ was to witness in the process of rescuing them.[27]

The second point in Hebrews concerns Melchisedech. This figure in Hebrews is never described as a type of Christ, is not reckoned with the angels, but is delineated as 'without father or mother or genealogy, and has neither beginning of days nor end of life, but resembling the Son of God he continues a priest for ever'. A figure who apparently has eternal being must either be a rival to Christ or be Christ himself. In my book *Jesus Christ in the Old Testament*, I argued that the author did in fact identify Melchisedech with an appearance of the pre-existent Christ, but did not quite have the nerve to say so explicitly (see Heb. 5.11–14).[28] Curiously enough, Dunn's language would suggest that he might be quite favourable to this idea. He writes that Melchisedech in Hebrews may be 'an embodiment of the Logos'.[29] But if this is the case, then surely we do have in Hebrews an example of personal pre-existence. Melchisedech is for the author an historical figure; indeed he represents the pre-existent Christ appearing in Israel's history, exactly what Dunn claims does not occur before the time of Justin.

Now we must carry the argument into Paul's own works, at the very passage where Dunn most emphatically denies that there is any trace of the doctrine of the pre-existent Christ active in Israel's history. This is I Corinthians 10.1–11. I will cite verses 1–4:

I want you to know, brethren, that our fathers were all under the cloud and all passed through the sea and all were baptised into Moses in the cloud and in the sea, and all ate the same supernatural (*pneumatikon*) food and all drank the same supernatural drink. For they drank from the supernatural Rock which followed them, and the Rock was Christ.

We should also note verse 11:

Now these things happened to them as a warning (*tupikōs*), but they were written down for our instruction, upon whom the end of the ages has come.

On the face of it, this looks like a retrojection of Christ into Israel's history. But Dunn attempts to explain it in terms of allegory and what he thinks is typology in such a way that Paul is represented as making no statement about Christ's activity in the past, only about what past events indicated concerning the historical Christ. Those events, he writes, 'happened to the Israelites typologically, but were written down for our instruction. . . . But is it an allegory of the realities then operative, or something more in the line of a typological allegory of the spiritual realities now experienced by the Corinthians?'[30] He opts for the latter alternative: 'baptized by Moses in the cloud and in the sea' is a parallel to 'baptized into Christ'. . . . 'Moses served as the typological counterpart of Christ . . . the manna from heaven and the water from the rock were simply types of the spiritual sustenance received by Christians from Christ'. He goes on to say that in the first half of the passage it was not necessary to identify Moses as the type of Christ; it was obvious. But the type of Christ had to be identified in the second half: 'Paul's readers should see the rock then as the type of Christ now'.[31]

The phrase 'the rock was (*ēn*) Christ' naturally causes some difficulty to this exposition. One would expect the present tense; as in Galatians 4.25: 'Now Hagar is Mount Sinai in Arabia.' But Dunn has his explanation for this: 'The imperfect tense, "the rock was Christ" is usually taken to rule out this interpretation (Dunn's), since elsewhere the interpretative key is given in the present tense (CD 6.4; Gal. 4.24f; II Cor. 3.17) . . . But in each of the cases cited that which is interpreted allegorically is something which was present to the interpreter there and then (the well, Hagar of Sinai, the veil, "the same veil", II Cor. 3.14); whereas the rock belonged exclusively to the past. "Was," therefore, not because Christ was there in the past, but because the rock is *not* in the present'.[32]

It seems to me that Dunn is here confusing typology and allegory in a way which only serves to darken counsel. Typology is the tracing of a pattern of events in the old dispensation that is reproduced in the new. Allegory means identifying some one feature or features in the Old Testament and declaring that they really signify something quite different to that which their literal meaning would suggest. Thus Philo can say that Moses giving water from the rock really means the Logos supplying divine wisdom to the initiated. Paul is using typology here, not allegory.[33] Hence we cannot translate the epithet *pneumatikon* in this passage with 'allegorical', as Dunn appears to wish to do. There is no such thing as 'allegorical' food or drink. Paul believed that the Israelites really ate and drank. By *pneumatikon* here he means 'coming from a supernatural source', very much as the RSV renders it.

Next, Dunn appears to have got his typology rather confused also. If Moses was the type of Christ when the Israelites crossed the Red Sea, he must have been the type of Christ also in providing the manna and the water from the rock. Hence we have the situation that at the giving of the water from the rock there are three elements: Moses (type of Christ if you like, though I think it confusing to put it this way), the water provided, and the provider, the rock, which stands for Christ in the same way that the pillar of cloud stands for Christ at the crossing of the Red Sea, not as the surrogate for an absent Christ who had not yet come into existence, but as the medium or means by which the then present Christ exercised his supernatural power. Paul is, in fact, being true to his position as outlined in Gal. 3.19–20: there the old order of the law is stigmatized as being indirect: it needs intermediaries (angels) and a mediator (Moses). The same situation prevails at the Red Sea and in the desert. Christ is present at both, in the pillar of cloud and in the rock, as the source of the supernatural deliverance, but Moses the mediator is also needed. He has to lift up his rod over the sea and strike the rock.

Typology does not infer that the events in the old dispensation were non-events, as allegory often does. In this passage Paul means that the events of the Red Sea and of the desert exhibited the pattern of the divine redemptive action; that pattern could be seen, more clearly because the action was now direct and unmediated, in the new order which the Corinthians could experience. The events happened *typikōs*, according to the pattern of God's design; they were recorded so that we could recognize that pattern.

'The rock was Christ.' Dunn's argument seems to me to be quite ineffective here. The rock, he claims, is different from the other types used by either Paul or Qumran because it is definitely in the past in a sense in which the others are not. He cites first CD 6.4, the 'Zadokite Document', where the well mentioned in Numbers 21.18 is associated with various stages in the history of the Sect: 'The well is the law, and those who dug it were the converts of Israel.'[34] At first glance, this looks like a triumphant vindication of Dunn; but, in fact, it is only Vermes' translation of the Hebrew, where there is no copula at all. The two elements of type and thing typified are simply put in apposition.[35] Now I cannot see how in respect of pastness the well in the Zadokite Document differs from the rock in I Corinthians 10.4. Both are part of the furniture of the desert period and have passed away. It is true, of course, that it is still possible to call the Torah 'a well of life'. But then it is still possible to describe Christ as a rock: 'Rock of ages, cleft for me'. Dunn's next example is taken from Gal. 4.24f.: 'Now Hagar is Mount Sinai in Arabia'. But Hagar has passed away, and is no more present than is the rock. Perhaps it is his third example that has really inspired Dunn's interpretation: the veil which in Exodus 34 Moses was described as placing on his face is in II Cor. 3.14 described as in some sense remaining today: 'that same veil remains unlifted, because only through Christ is it taken away'. But a moment's reflection will show that Paul does not mean this literally. He does not mean that the same veil which Moses put on his face is found today on the hearts of Jews. A literal historical veil in old times points to a metaphorical, allegorical veil today. Thus Paul here is doing the opposite of allegorizing the Old Testament; he is allegorizing the present position of the Jews. In any case, this gives us no justification for maintaining that the words 'the rock was Christ' are to be taken in anything but their obvious meaning: 'in, with and under' that rock as the supernatural source of drink. What the phrase cannot mean is: 'that rock at the time indicated that Christ was to do something similar hundreds of years later' or, more grotesque still 'the rock which was there now indicates that Christ is the source of supernatural sustenance to believers'.

We may point to one more important piece of evidence in favour of the view that Paul is referring in this passage to the activity of the pre-existent Christ. The RSV translates I Cor. 10.9 thus:

We must not put the Lord to the test, as some of them did.

Dunn would presumably understand 'the Lord' here as God, not Christ, though it is more likely on the evidence that 'the Lord' means Christ. However, there is a very well attested variant reading here 'we must not put Christ (*ton Christon*) to the test'. If this is correct, Dunn's case collapses completely: Paul must be referring to the pre-existent Christ. As for the probability of the reading *ton Christon*, I cannot do better than quote G. G. Zunz in his magisterial Schweich Lectures:

'kurion' ('Lord'), said Th. Zahn, 'ought never again to be printed in the text'. It is in all critical editions from Lachmann down to von Soden and Merk. No evidence prior to the fourth century can be quoted for it. What evidence for it exists comes from Egypt, whence later on the variant spread to Ethiopia and, via Syria ('Euthalius') to Armenia; yet the Egyptian versions, borne out by Clement and now also by P[46], demonstrate that originally it was not read in Egypt either; nor was it in Palestine, where Origen and later Fathers based christological arguments on the opposite variant. The latter is attested from the second century onward and everywhere from Lyons to Edessa, not excepting Alexandria. Under these circumstances to accept the reading *kurion* is *fides non quaerens intellectum*. The reading *Christon* was apt to stir speculation: how could the Jews in the desert have tempted Christ? The difficulty is removed by the reading 'Lord' which left open the reference to the God of the Old Testament. If the latter reading had been original, no one would have cared to create difficulty by the uncalled-for gloss 'Christ'. *Kurion* then is a (later) Alexandrian corruption, which had a very limited effect upon the tradition in general.[36]

Dunn's arguments grow more and more improbable as he works his way through the Pauline corpus. At Romans 10.6–7 he has to argue against the obvious conclusion that Paul is referring to the coming down of Christ from heaven followed by his descent into Hades when he writes 'Do not say in your heart "Who will ascend into heaven?" (that is, to bring Christ down) or "Who will descend into the abyss?" (that is, to bring Christ up from the dead)'. Dunn offers the following paraphrase: 'though Christ is distant from those still on earth (he has ascended into heaven as he has already descended to the abyss), righteousness is still possible. For righteousness is not to be attained by bringing Christ back on earth.' This is going against the natural order, and also introduces an element quite foreign to the context. Paul is here arguing that righteousness has been brought to us by God in Christ, as against the Jewish claim that it is to be found by following the Torah. No one has ever suggested that Christ should be brought back to earth, and Dunn only brings in the thought in order to make his interpretation more probable, not because the context requires it.

However, Dunn attains the height of implausibility when he reaches Colossians. He actually undertakes the Herculean task of trying to show that there is no real doctrine of pre-existence in Colossians 1.15–20. It is hardly necessary to reproduce his arguments. In the face of such statements as 'in him all things were created' and 'he is before all things' and 'he is the beginning', it would seem impossible to believe that we do not have a doctrine of pre-existence here. But Dunn gallantly maintains his thesis. This he does by means of a series of paraphrases which prove, if they are correct, that the author of Colossians was using language in a purely Pickwickian sense. The phrase 'the firstborn of all creation' is explained thus: 'he, through whom God already recognizable in his creation becomes understandable'.[37] The words 'in him all things were created' really mean, it seems, 'This may simply be the writer's way of saying that Christ now reveals the character of the power behind the world'.[38] He also attempts an analogy, which he takes from the career of Sir Harold Wilson: 'Prime Minister Wilson studied Economics at Oxford. No one misunderstands the phrase to mean that Harold Wilson was already Prime Minister when he was at Oxford (though this is the most "natural" meaning of the sentence) . . . Paul's readers could obviously make the same paraphrase without difficulty: By wisdom, that later "became" Christ Jesus, all things were created.'[39] But the Harold Wilson who studied Economics at Oxford is one and the same being as the Harold Wilson who later became Prime Minister. If Dunn admits the force of the analogy, he has betrayed his own case. The truth is that, if he had wished to make his theory less implausible (though I do not think that in any circumstances it can be anything but unconvincing), he should have abandoned the Pauline authorship of Colossians. One simply cannot hold without danger of absurdity both that Paul wrote Colossians and that Paul had no doctrine of Christ's pre-existence.

I conclude therefore that Paul did hold a doctrine of Christ's pre-existence and that we are justified in using it as an analogy in the next chapter. It is not difficult to see how he could have come to formulate this doctrine. Dunn is no doubt right in saying that contemporary Judaism had not actually reached the conception of a personal pre-existent being. But the concept of the divine wisdom comes close to it, as Dunn demonstrates; and to this we can add a feature which he omits – the way in which in the Book of Wisdom chapter 10 the divine wisdom is represented as accompanying the patriarchs through their wandering, and the Israelites in the exodus and the desert sojourn, very much as Paul, the author of Hebrews, and the author of the Fourth Gospel represent the pre-existent Christ as doing. As well as this, there was the concept of the heavenly man, which Paul must have learned from Alexandrian Judaism, though not necessarily directly from Philo. I discuss this in slightly more detail in the next chapter. The reason why Paul was moved to formulate this doctrine is not far to seek: he wished to fit Jesus Christ into salvation history. The story of a man who lived for thirty years, was the Messiah, died and rose again was not in itself sufficient explanation of how Jesus Christ fitted into God's plan for the world. Nor does it help to say, as Dunn in effect does, that through the resurrection he became God, or was identified with God. A crude adoptionism such as this is would not have seemed adequate to Paul. In order to explain the full soteriological significance of Jesus Paul was constrained to formulate a doctrine of Christ's pre-existence.

The reader will be aware that, though I defend the claim that Paul had a doctrine of pre-existence, I do not follow precisely that doctrine in my own approach to the incarnation. I do not think that the way in which the New Testament writers presented the doctrine of pre-existence is tenable by us today, and I sympathize with Dunn, inasmuch as he holds the same conviction. My reasons are given in detail in the next chapter. Indeed his sustained denial of such a doctrine to Paul in the teeth of the evidence, as it seems to me, is no doubt ultimately motivated by a very laudable desire to find a doctrine of the incarnation which avoids some of the difficulties presented by the traditional account of that doctrine. But, if we are to make such an attempt (and I have no doubt that we must, since I have done so), it must be based on the witness of the New Testament as it actually is, not just as we would like it to be. And I think there can be very little doubt that the doctrine of the personal pre-existence of Christ is to be found in the genuine Pauline writings, in Colossians, in the Epistle to the Hebrews, and in the Fourth Gospel. In three of these four sources Christ's pre-existent activity in Israel's history is also implied.

Four

The Analogy of Pre-existence

In Chapter 2 I rejected the argument, suggested by Professor C. F. D. Moule, that in effect post-existence implies pre-existence, that the New Testament writers came to attribute a pre-incarnational status to Jesus because they experienced him after his resurrection, as one who transcended temporal limits. Still less of course are we today justified in using this argument. But pre-existence is a large and important element in the christology of the three greatest theologians in the New Testament, Paul, the author of Hebrews, and John. We cannot ignore it and we cannot deny that it has some connection with post-existence. In this chapter I begin by examining Paul's doctrine of pre-existence in some detail, then turn to that of Hebrews and of John, and finally propose that, though the doctrine as set forth in Paul and Hebrews cannot serve as our model in christology, we can derive from it a useful analogy for how best we can express the post-existence of Jesus, that is, his relation to God and to us since his resurrection.

We must begin by observing that there is some interesting evidence in early rabbinic literature about the possibility of man seeing God.[1] The Old Testament scriptures certainly represent this as having taken place on several occasions: in Genesis 32, Jacob wrestles with an angel and afterwards declares 'I have seen God face to face'. Moses is granted a vision of God in the burning bush in Exodus 3. In the narrative of Exodus 24.9–11 Moses, Aaron, and the elders of Israel ascend the holy mount and 'they saw the God of Israel'. Later, the skin of Moses' face is described as shining because he had been talking to God in the tabernacle. There is the incident of the challenge to Moses' authority by Aaron and Miriam in Numbers 12.1–8, where God is represented as saying: 'With Moses I speak mouth to mouth . . . and he beholds the form of the Lord.' We have Isaiah's famous vision of the Lord of hosts in the temple narrated in Isaiah 6.1–5: 'I saw the Lord sitting upon a throne.' And above all there is Ezekiel's great vision of God narrated in Ezekiel 1, which culminates in the words 'and seated above the likeness of a throne was a likeness as it were of a human form'. These examples could not be denied by Jewish exegetic tradition, but they could cause embarrassment, especially after Israel had had to meet the challenge of Greek philosophy with its strong conviction that God did not belong to the realm of the visible.

The general sentiment of rabbinic comment was that no man can expect to see God in this present age, though in the age to come the righteous will see him. There are various instances of Gentiles demanding to see God and rabbis responding by telling them to look directly at the sun. The implication is that God cannot be seen because of his exceeding glory not necessarily because he is metaphysically incapable of being revealed in the world of particulars. The natural conclusion is that if anyone in the past has seen God, it cannot have been God in his essence who was seen, but an image of God. When it came to expounding the texts in which God is described as having been seen, Jewish exegesis resorted to periphrasis: in Num. 12.6–8 the Targum of Pseudo-Jonathan says that Moses 'beheld the likeness of my Shekinah'. Nearly all translations or paraphrases of Exodus 24.10–11 qualify the absoluteness of the original Hebrew text. The Septuagint offers: 'they saw the place where God . . . stood'. Symmachus renders: 'they saw God . . . in a vision'; Josephus, in his account of Jacob's wrestling in Gen. 32, says he wrestled with 'a phantom', suggesting thereby that the whole thing was a dream (*Ant.* I. 331–2). Sometimes distinctions are drawn as to the degree of clarity with which various people in Israel's history saw God: 'All the prophets looked into a dim glass but Moses looked through a clear glass.'[2] In Tractate Hagiga 13b[3] an unfavourable contrast is drawn between Ezekiel and Isaiah: Ezekiel is like a villager who saw the king. Isaiah is like a townsman who saw the king: i.e. the villagers, being illiterate, had to give a great deal more detail of his vision in order to be believed.

This vision described in Ezekiel 1, often referred to as the 'chariot vision', gave considerable anxiety to the Rabbis. They were afraid of anthropomorphism, perhaps of the danger of idolatry, and it is quite possible that in the second and third centuries of the Christian era they were cautious about dealing with it because Christians were claiming that it was a vision of the pre-existent Christ. Jervell brings evidence to show that according to some Rabbis what Ezekiel saw was a heavenly image, *eikōn*, which was identified with Israel.[4] This is the suggestion that when God appears as man he appears both as the image of himself and as the image of ideal humanity. There is an interesting passage in *Pesikta Rabbati* in which God is represented as cataloguing the various human guises in which he appeared to Israel of old: as a warrior at the Red Sea; as an elder teaching Torah on Sinai; as a bridegroom entering the marriage chamber in the tabernacle.[5] Thus there is in the Judaism of the first three centuries of our era a tradition that, when anyone in scripture is described as having seen God, he must have seen the image of God, and probably that image took the form of a man.

I have already dealt with J. D. G. Dunn's rejection of this thesis. He has his own exposition of II Corinthians.[6] The great majority of scholars agree that Paul did have a doctrine of the pre-existent Christ. Several, such as Cullmann and Käsemann, insist that Paul's interest in the pre-existent Christ was more functional than ontological, and this we freely admit.[7] We might note Eltester's conclusion: 'The *eikōn* of God is a sort of heavenly being', and Jervell's dictum that in Paul the *doxa* (glory) of God and the *eikōn* of God are synonymous.[8] R. P. Martin, in his extremely able treatment of the 'hymn of the incarnation' in Philippians 2.1–11, writes of 'the pre-temporal existence of the heavenly Lord in his unique relationship to God'.[9] And R. G. Hammerton-Kelly in his study of the pre-existence conception emphasizes that Paul believed in a pre-existent being whom he identified with Jesus Christ.[10]

But what was Christ like, according to Paul, in this pre-incarnational existence? We can find some light on this question by a consideration of Paul's description of Christ as 'the man from heaven' and 'the man of heaven' (better 'heavenly man') in I Cor. 15.47, 49. We know of a similar conception from Paul's senior contemporary, Philo of Alexandria. Philo clearly distinguishes between the two creation accounts in Genesis, found respectively in chapters 1 and 2. The account in chapter 1, he says, gives us a description of the 'heavenly man' (exactly Paul's phrase in I Cor. 15.49). He, who is also called 'ideal man', is the true image of God because he has no part in the temporal or earthly. The creation account in Genesis 2 refers to empirical or earthly man and is of course identical with Adam. Philo associates his heavenly man closely with the Word of God, the Logos, which plays a big part in his philosophy, though it is not clear whether he actually identifies his 'heavenly man' with the Logos. Scholars are very much divided on the question as to whether Paul knew of Philo's conception of the heavenly man or not. Paul does not generally speaking betray a knowledge of Philo's works elsewhere in his writings, and it seems safer to conclude that Paul was acquainted with speculations about 'a heavenly original Man' in Hellenized Judaism;[11] he was not consciously modifying Philo's scheme. What is important is to insist that, according to Paul, Christ did not only begin to be the heavenly man at the resurrection. Though Paul calls him 'the last Adam' and 'the second man' (I Cor. 15.45, 47), he does not mean that he only became last Adam or heavenly man either at the incarnation or at the resurrection: He always was the heavenly man. This is denied by Dunn who writes: 'Christ's rôle as "second man" does not begin either in some pre-existent state or at incarnation.'[12] I find this impossible to reconcile with Paul's statement in I Cor. 15.47 that 'the second man is from heaven' and very difficult to reconcile with Paul's calling Christ the 'heavenly man' two verses later. I agree with Dunn that the era of the Spirit only began at the resurrection, in Paul's view, but I see nothing incongruous in the suggestion that Paul thought of Christ as the heavenly man from all eternity, to be described as 'the second man' because he was only revealed as such at the resurrection. I can quote Jervell, R. P. Martin, and C. K. Barrett in defence of this view.[13] Christ's quality of being the image of God was not confined to the period of the incarnation, though it was uniquely revealed during that period. He was also revealed as image during Israel's history, as narrated in scripture. And he now exists as God's image to be apprehended by faith in the experience of the church.

We are now able to take the final step and to suggest that according to Paul the pre-existent Christ whenever he revealed himself appeared in human form. This is implied by Cullmann when he writes: 'Jesus the divine, heavenly man was divine already in his pre-existence.'[14] Larsson writes similarly that 'the man from heaven' cannot apply only to the parousia; it must apply also to the earthly life and to Christ's origin in the heavenly world. In fact it must be attributed to 'the fact of Christ in toto'.[15] It is interesting in this context to note the evidence produced by Jervell to show that in rabbinic tradition unfallen Adam had a supra-human appearance: 'Adam was a figure of light. His face shone brighter than the sun.'[16] This gives us some idea of how Paul must have thought of the pre-existent Christ.

An objection to this conclusion might be brought on the grounds that in Philippians 2.7 Paul, referring specifically to the life of the historical Jesus, uses the phrase 'being born in the likeness of men'. If Christ as image of both God and man always existed in human form, how can he be described as 'being born in the likeness of men', or indeed in the next verse as 'being found in human form'? We may reply in the first place that the words are probably not original to Paul but part of the hymn which he is here quoting. In any case, any doctrine that regards the pre-existent Christ as liable to appear on occasions in the course of Israel's history must imply both that the pre-existent being could appear in human form (e.g. to Abraham at the oaks of Mamre, Gen. 18) and that his appearance as Jesus of Nazareth on the stage of history for thirty years had something unique about it. Indeed the suggestion that in Paul's view the pre-existent Christ appeared in human form goes a considerable way towards solving the question, how can he be at one and the same time the pre-existent image of God and the pre-existent image of man? Because, Paul would reply, God chose that at various points in Israel's history he should be manifested through the pre-existent Christ in the form of a man. We think of all the theophanies listed at the beginnings of this chapter, starting from the three men at the oaks of Mamre and culminating in Ezekiel's mysterious vision of God 'in the likeness as it were of a human form'. Christ was the form in which God was known to Israel of old, and that form, in so far as it was visible, was the form of a man. In my article I go on to argue that, according to Paul in II Cor. 3, it was the pre-existent Christ who appeared to Moses in the tabernacle; but we do not need to pursue this argument any further.

We should now be in a position to sketch Paul's doctrine of the incarnation, as far as it can be known to us. There always existed, Paul would say, an eternal being beside God the Father whom he can call the Son, but can on occasion simply refer to as Jesus Christ (e.g. II Cor. 8.9). He existed in the form of 'the heavenly man', and appeared on various occasions in Israel's history as the manifestation of God's presence in the form of a man. He always represented God active for salvation and whenever God appeared to chosen people in Israel, Abraham, Moses, the prophets, it was in this form that he appeared. But we should not think of this 'form of a man' as in any way approximating to an incarnation. It was more like an angelophany and there is no suggestion that in the pre-incarnational period the 'heavenly man' had any of the limitations of humanity. These appearances, however, did represent a genuine, though incomplete, revelation of God.

Then came the incarnation: the Son of God was born of a woman as Jesus Christ, lived a life of faith not works, voluntarily submitted to die on the cross according to the Father's will, and did so die. There are traces of Jesus' teaching reproduced in Paul, so Paul must have attributed some value to the details of this incarnate life. But he gives us almost no clues as to how he thinks Jesus lived. I have included in this brief account all that I think can be gathered from Paul. One might perhaps add that the Son in his life, death, and resurrection underwent the experience of salvation, not from sin but from ultimate annihilation by the powers of evil.[17] He died according to God's will revealed in the scriptures. He descended into the underworld.[18] On the third day he was raised from the dead by the power of God, appeared to his disciples (including Paul) and convinced them that he was now alive and available for the faithful in the realm of the Spirit. God has exalted him, in the sense that he is now revealed as Son of God and heavenly man and victor over the powers of evil. He will come again quite soon and at that time those who believe in him will also enter that spiritual realm and be given 'spiritual bodies' which will enable them to share fully in the life of the risen Christ. Through this process of incarnation and resurrection God has communicated himself to mankind, both because he has now in the incarnation, culminating in the cross, revealed his character fully as one of self-giving love, and because he has carried out his great eschatological act of salvation whereby all men, not Israel only, are called into saving fellowship with him through Christ in the Spirit. We should observe that, though Paul has his doctrine of the church as the body of Christ, he does not talk in terms of 'glorified humanity' or 'manhood seated at the right hand of God'.

He certainly believes that we can know the risen Christ by faith now and will know him even better at the parousia when we will receive 'spiritual bodies', but I believe that the conception of deified humanity did not form part of his thought.

Hebrews apparently presents us with a similar, though by no means identical, doctrine. The first chapter of the Epistle makes it quite clear that the author has a doctrine of the pre-existent Christ. He does not seem as free as Paul is in applying the name 'Jesus Christ' to the pre-existent being. He uses the terms *apaugasma* ('reflection') and *charaktēr* ('facsimile'), but these can hardly be regarded as names for the pre-existent being. It is not even certain that the name 'Son' is unhesitatingly applied by him to the pre-existent state. Hebrews 1.2 could be rendered: 'he has in the last days spoken to us in the mode of Son', which would imply that the sonship only began at the incarnation. And if, as seems very probable, the name referred to in 1.4 is 'Son', the author says that the pre-existent one has inherited it, has had it conferred on him. He did not apparently hold it always. Indeed it may be that if we could challenge the author of Hebrews as to what name he applies to the pre-existent being, he would answer 'Lord', or even conceivably 'God' (see 1.8). It can also be shown that Hebrews, like Paul, believed that the pre-existent Lord appeared at various points in Israel's history.[19]

We have more information about how the author of Hebrews viewed the Jesus of the incarnation. He was fully man; he lived by faith – indeed he is the great exemplar of faith. He learned obedience by suffering. Though sinless he was not immune to temptation. He exhibited fully human emotions. He genuinely prayed to God to be freed from ultimate death, and God heard his prayer because of his deep devotion.[20] The way in which God heard his prayer was by raising him from the dead. Jesus now lives for ever in heaven as exalted Son, where he continually makes intercession for us on the basis of his perfect sacrifice. He can be called 'the great shepherd of the sheep' (13.20), so he has a direct relation to the faithful which transcends that of just a living example, though this it certainly is. Moule points out that Hebrews does not seem to have a corporate conception of the risen and ascended Christ, as Paul and John have.[21] Hence the question of the body of Christ or the 'glorified humanity' simply does not occur in his work. His flesh, it is true, is compared to the veil before the holy of holies in 10.20; but that veil has been passed through and he now stands in the presence of God for us.

We observe that neither Paul nor the author of Hebrews has made any real attempt to relate Jesus Christ ontologically to God. Hebrews comes nearest to it in his magnificent opening paragraph, but he never elaborates his hints given in the words *apaugasma* and *charaktēr*. It might be said of both Paul and Hebrews that they were so much interested in Christ's work that they did not give themselves time to complete an account of his person. It was otherwise with Colossians and the Fourth Gospel. I discuss Colossians more fully below, contenting myself here with saying that, though Colossians has not found a satisfactory name for the pre-existent being, he has gone farther than Paul in relating him to God and to the cosmos. The great difference with John is that he, benefitting no doubt from the experience of his predecessors, has found a satisfactory name and concept for the pre-existent being. He calls him the Word, and presents a Logos doctrine. This must be his own deliberate choice and no mere use of traditional vocabulary. It means that John could now place the doctrine of the incarnation in an intelligible framework. It has immensely far-reaching effects. It means that the Fourth Gospel was concentrated far more on the being of Jesus than on his work. It also meant that the church now had a firm basis on which to build its doctrine of the incarnation. This was not however pure gain. R. E. Brown is fully justified when he writes: 'Johannine christology has nurtured a widespread unconscious monophysitism, popular even today, in which Jesus is not really like us in everything except sin, but omniscient, unable to suffer or be tempted, foreseeing the whole future.'[22] Presently we must ask ourselves how John related the Logos to Jesus Christ.

Why did these writers, Paul, John, the authors of Hebrews and Colossians, present Jesus Christ in this way? Why did they in effect elaborate a doctrine of the incarnation? We cannot claim that God incarnate was an original datum of experience, and the synoptic gospels show no clear signs of a desire to present a doctrine of an incarnation. Nor can we plead some sort of development of religious thought, as if christology moves from the primitive ideas of Mark, through Luke, Matthew, Paul, and Hebrews till it reaches its climax in John. Paul probably died before any of the synoptic gospels was published, and there is no reason at all to suggest either that Hebrews must have been written after Luke or Matthew, or that it was influenced by them. The puzzling fact is that the synoptic gospels, which as publications are later than Paul and contemporary with Hebrews, do not exhibit any tendency to elaborate a doctrine of pre-existence. The difference must lie in the different circumstances and mentalities of the respective authors. Paul was an intellectual, in touch with developments in Judaism, particularly perhaps the Judaism of the Diaspora. The author of Hebrews must have had some touch with Alexandrian Judaism. The author of Colossians was a disciple of Paul, facing a form of divergent teaching which gave an important place to cosmology. John not only benefitted from the experience of his predecessors, but also belonged to a tradition which was at close quarters with contemporary Judaism and contemporary Hellenistic religious speculation.

But the ultimate reason why Paul and the author of Hebrews at least worked out a doctrine of incarnation was that they had a concern for salvation history, the story of God's dealings with his people and with mankind. They were sufficiently intellectuals to realize that it would not permanently be sufficient to claim that in Jesus God had brought about his eschatological salvation and revealed his full nature, as he always said he would in the last days. In any case the last days seemed to be continued in a way which traditional eschatological belief had not allowed for. Jews would ask how this new revelation of God was related to the old, and Gentiles would ask why God had retained his revelation until these last days. Both Paul and the author of Hebrews had inherited a tradition which claimed that Jesus had fulfilled the scriptures. It is therefore natural that Christian intellectuals should search the scriptures (which of course were what we call the Old Testament) in order to find traces of Jesus. And from that it was not a great step to conclude that in some form Jesus could be found active in the history of God's people of old. This was a great relief as far as a doctrine of revelation was concerned, and both Paul and Hebrews have as their basic assumption the belief that God has spoken in Jesus (Heb. 1.1–2), has commended his love towards us in Christ (Rom. 5.8). It meant that the incarnation need not be looked on as a divine intrusion, a mere incident in the dealings of God with man, integrally unrelated to anything that went before. On the contrary, what has now become apparent in the life of Jesus Christ, they could argue, has had precedents, foreshadowings. God always was as he is now known to be in Christ, and had even in some measure manifested himself as such of old. If we take an even wider perspective, we can say that the doctrine of Christ's pre-existent activity in Israel's history was the best way available to early Christians of making the sacred book of Judaism their own.

It should be emphasized that this doctrine of pre-existence did not prejudice the reality and uniqueness of the incarnation. As I have pointed out already, the appearances in the course of Israel's history were often more like angelophanies. Paul apparently can envisage the pre-existent Christ appearing in the pillar of cloud as the Israelites crossed the Red Sea (I Cor. 10.1). And I have argued above that the author of Hebrews actually identified Melchisedech with an appearance of the pre-existent Christ.[23] It will become clear presently that there is reason to believe that John identified the pre-existent Logos with one of the angels who visited Abraham at the oaks of Mamre. All New Testament writers who show traces of this doctrine would emphasize the superiority of the incarnation over all pre-incarnate appearances: it was direct, much closer to humanity, continuous, climactic, normative, permanent in its effects. And I would also add that the desire to fit Jesus into salvation history was not the only motive behind the elaboration of the doctrine of pre-existence: it depended on the experience which Christians had of the risen Christ in the church; and the Wisdom tradition helped to make it possible. But these last two factors were necessary conditions rather than activating impulses. The pre-existence doctrine began, I believe, as an attempt to make sense of the career of Jesus in the light of *all* God's dealings with his people. Cullmann and Käsemann are quite right to insist that Paul's interest in the pre-existent Christ was more functional than ontological.[24] The doctrine was in its own way a necessary attempt to work out a philosophy of religion, to relate God's action in Christ to all that was known of God and his ways.

I have suggested that in Colossians and the Fourth Gospel the doctrine of pre-existence is extended so as to form a basis for relating Jesus to God on an ontological basis. This does not mean that the element of salvation history is dropped, certainly not in John at least.[25] This new development was an answer to a contemporary challenge: in the church in Colossae some people were teaching that Christ had a subordinate position with respect to God and the cosmos. In John's community the Jews were opposing the doctrine of 'the two powers', the claim that in Jesus Christ God had been uniquely manifested. Both these writers therefore consciously present a christology which relates Christ to God as a hypostasis within the godhead, to use later language. Thus, what we might call a Logos doctrine only came when the situation called it out. Nobody that we know of in the early church indulged in theological speculation simply for the fun of it. We are not justified, therefore, either in condemning the author of Colossians and John for arbitrarily introducing Hellenistic speculations into an originally pure and simple gospel, or in claiming that the doctrine of the incarnation of the Word of God was an original datum of experience, taught by Jesus himself and handed on by the earliest disciples.

There is a reasonable parallel to be drawn here with the evolution of the doctrine of the Trinity. No responsible New Testament scholar would claim that the doctrine of the Trinity was taught by Jesus, or preached by the earliest Christians, or consciously held by any writer in the New Testament. It was in fact slowly worked out in the course of the first few centuries in an attempt to give an intelligible doctrine of God. It was inevitable that Christian thinkers should begin from God and work out the relation of the Son and the Spirit to the Father afterwards. It was not at all surprising that until the time of Origen all Christian theologians should hold a purely 'economic' doctrine of the Trinity: the three Persons were part of God's 'economy' in dealing with the world and had not always existed in distinction. It was also extremely natural that the Father should be seen as the 'fount of godhead' and retain a sort of superiority not really justified by the requirements of the doctrine itself. The doctrine of the Trinity developed along heuristic lines. But the final result, as expressed for example in the *Quicunque Vult*, does more justice to the doctrine of God as Three in One than do many earlier versions of the Trinity.

So with the doctrine of the incarnation: we can see why it began with great emphasis on the pre-existent appearances of Christ, but we can also see why this element afterwards fell into the background. Once a Logos doctrine (not necessarily John's Logos doctrine in every respect) had been proposed, the relation of Jesus to God could be considered on a quasi-philosophical basis; the whole question of the relation of the Word to Jesus could be looked at in a new light; the challenge that Christians believed in two gods could be rebutted. The fact that a Logos-doctrine came later in the New Testament period does not mean that it was necessarily a corruption or an undesirable development. It could mean that the problem was now being viewed in its full proportions.

We have still to examine as far as we can the pre-existence doctrine of Colossians and the Fourth Gospel respectively. We have observed that these two differ from their predecessors in that both are consciously relating Christ to God and to the cosmos. Colossians is particularly interesting because it has what is virtually a Logos doctrine without using the word Logos. Perhaps if there is a name for the pre-existent being in Colossians, it is *eikōn*. The famous incarnation passage in Col. 1.15–19 begins with the phrase 'who is the image (*eikōn*) of the invisible God'. Scholars have pointed out that this beginning with 'who' is the sign that a hymn is being quoted. Obvious parallels are Phil. 2.6 and I Tim. 3.16. What is more, there is no name to be a subject of 'who' in Col. 1.15. The nearest noun occurs in v. 13 'the Son of his love', which suggests that perhaps the author of Colossians would have used the Pauline title 'Son' for the pre-existent being. What is clear is that he does not write 'Jesus is the image of the invisible God, in Jesus all things were created, and hold together, etc.'

There are a number of striking parallels between this passage and Philo's Logos doctrine. Philo calls his Logos *prōtogonos* ('first begotten'), which corresponds to *prōtotokos* ('first-born') in Col. 1.15. Philo's Logos is described as 'the bond of all things' which reminds us of 'in him all things hold together' of Col. 1.17. And Philo uses the words *eikōn* ('image') and *archē* ('beginning') of his Logos, just as the author of Colossians uses them of Christ in 1.15 and 1.18.[26] These resemblances, together with a number of other peculiarities in chapters 1–3, have convinced me that Colossians 1–3 was not written by Paul but by a disciple who knew his master's mind. He may even have been a closer disciple than was the author of Ephesians. Faced by the challenge of the new teaching in the church in Colossae, he has seen the need deliberately to work out the relationship of the pre-existent Lord to God and has gone to Philo for help in this. But he has not used Philo's actual term Logos, perhaps because he does not want to appear to be a member of Philo's school.

The phrase 'the image of the invisible God' does not at first sight seem to bring us beyond what Paul says in II Cor. 4.4 where he describes Christ as 'the image of God'. And indeed the phrase in Col. 1.15 very adequately describes what Paul believed about Christ: he is the visibility, one might rather say the apprehensibility, of God. Whenever God has appeared it has in fact been Christ who was apprehended. But the epithet 'invisible' for God suggests that the author of Colossians has moved rather farther in the direction of a Greek conception of God than Paul was willing to go. In Greek thought God was transcendent, belonging essentially to the realm of thought, mind, contemplation, utterly removed from the things of sense. The implication of this phrase here is that in the Son we have as close an image of God as is possible within the realm of the visible. Paul's (and indeed John's) great contention was that in the Jesus Christ of history, and supremely in his cross, God has revealed himself so fully that he could not have manifested himself more clearly by any other means. The author of Colossians by stressing the invisibility of God has perhaps conceded rather too much to Philo, who says explicitly that his Logos, just because he has to involve himself in the events of history, is inferior to God and an inadequate representation of him.

But we may be misjudging the author of Colossians. After all John can emphasize that no man has ever seen God (1.18), but he never suggests that the Son as a revelation of God is in any way inferior. Calvin's comment on John 1.18b is perfectly just: in the Son, the Father has shown us the very secrets of his bosom. And in Colossians we have plenty of evidence that Christ is the full revelation of the Father: in him all the treasures of wisdom are to be found etc. So, though the author has, very reasonably in the circumstances, gone to Philo for help with his ontological problem, he has not allowed himself to be misled into Philo's ontological subordination of the Logos to God. We can use his splendid phrase 'image of the invisible God' to express satisfactorily how we envisage the relationship of the risen Christ to the Word.

When the author of Colossians calls the Son 'the image of the invisible God' he must mean it to apply to the Son in all three phases of his existence: he is the image of God in all God's appearances in Israel's history. He is supremely the image during the period of the incarnation. He is still the image now when he can only be known by faith. Philo uses the phrase 'manifest image of the invisible nature' of mankind,[27] and though we do not find the doctrine of Christ as the heavenly man explicitly stated in Colossians, it is safe to conclude that the author did see Christ as perfect man, both ideally in his pre-existent state and actually during the incarnation.

Is there then any trace of a doctrine of 'glorified humanity' in Colossians? No more, I believe, than there is in the authentic Pauline letters. Certainly the author inherits from Paul a corporate conception of the risen Christ. He wishes to present every man perfect in Christ (1.28). Christ's sufferings can in a mysterious way be supplemented by those of his servants (1.24). We have actually been raised with Christ in baptism (2.13). Because we have been raised together with Christ we must seek the things that are above, where Christ is seated at the right hand of God; and our life is hidden with Christ in God (3.1–3). But none of this, it seems to me, implies a doctrine of Christ's 'glorified humanity'. On the contrary, Christ is so closely associated with God, that there does not seem to be any scope for his humanity in his risen state. There is one aspect in which both Colossians and Ephesians differ from Paul here. Paul would not say, as these two epistles do, that we have already been raised with Christ. In Paul our resurrection is still in the future (see Rom. 6.5; 8.11; I Cor. 15.22). But this, in fact, makes the conception of a 'glorified humanity' even more inappropriate. If our present state is to be in some sense already raised with Christ, his 'glorified humanity' can have nothing to do with that. We are related to Christ as to the divine Word, not to a humanity existing somehow attached to the divine Word. It is much easier to envisage a 'glorified humanity' being somehow related to us in the hereafter, whose conditions are completely strange to us, than in our present state. Hence, the more either Colossians or the Fourth Gospel emphasizes realized eschatology the less room there is for any 'glorified humanity'.

We now turn to an examination of the Fourth Gospel to see if there are any traces of the two features which it seems so difficult to make sense of, a personal pre-existence of Jesus Christ, and a 'glorified humanity' belonging to the risen Lord. On the face of it we would not expect John explicitly to identify Jesus with the pre-existent Logos. He has deliberately taken the courageous step of using the term Logos for the pre-existing being, a term which no one ever has claimed was used by Jesus for himself. Whatever the origin of other christological terms, this one must be a construction. Since, therefore, John deliberately chose it in order to denote the pre-existent being, it would

seem unnecessary and confusing if he were to refer to the pre-existent
Jesus. Consequently we do not find any reference in John's prologue
to Jesus Christ until after he has come to his statement of the incarnation in 1.14. Immediately after that he represents the Baptist as witness-
ing to the pre-existence of the Word. The Baptist in the Fourth Gospel
stands for the tradition of believing Israel. In him the prophets are
summed up, so it is perfectly appropriate, from John's point of view
though not from that of the historical Baptist, that he should witness
to the Word's activities in Israel's history. I believe that this is what is
referred to in 1.16 'from his fullness have we all received, grace upon
grace'. Then in verse 17 comes the contrast between the old dispensation and the new: 'For the law was given through Moses; grace and
truth came through Jesus Christ.' John can now use the historical
name 'Jesus Christ' because he is referring to a process culminating
in the incarnation. It is very significant that the very next verse should
contain John's version of the phrase 'the image of the invisible
God'. The pre-existent Son[28] has always been the Father's image, but
supremely and decisively in the incarnation.

There is thus in the prologue to the Fourth Gospel nothing that
demands a doctrine of a pre-existent person called *Jesus* Christ, only of
the pre-existent Word of God, hypostasis of the godhead. But are there
any other references in the gospel that might suggest such a doctrine?
In 1.53 there is an unmistakeable reference to Jacob's vision at Bethel.
I believe that when the typology of this is worked out it can be shown
that the appearance of God in that vision in heaven at the top of the
ladder corresponds to the Son,[29] and it is significant that Jesus is
represented as saying that the angels are to ascend and descend upon
'the Son of Man' not upon Jesus Christ. In other words, Jacob's vision
was of the Son, the divine Word rather than of a person called Jesus
Christ. Again in 8.39–40 Jesus is represented as saying to the Jews:
'If you were Abraham's children, you would do what Abraham did,
but now you seek to kill me, a man (*anthrōpon*) who has told you the
truth which I heard from God; this is not what Abraham did.' In view
of Jesus' claim in 8.56–58 that Abraham saw his day, and that before
Abraham existed he was, we may reasonably conclude that a claim is
being made in 8.39–40 concerned with the Word's pre-existence. In
other words, just as Jesus is a man who is telling the Jews the truth he
learned from God, so it was in Abraham's time. The pre-existent

Word was one of those who told Abraham the truth he learned from God. This means that John can use *anthrōpos* (man) to denote an appearance of the pre-existent Word. But, as we have seen in the case of Paul, this does not at all imply that the pre-existent Word was a man. He appeared in the form of man as God's image. It is, of course, true that the historical Jesus here is represented as having existed before the incarnation and taken part in Israel's history. But John could hardly have depicted the historical Jesus as having said: 'As the Word of God I visited Abraham.' He has gone as far as he could, far beyond the bounds of historical probability, in representing a Jesus who is conscious of pre-existence. He cannot be expected to provide his Jesus with a complete ready-made christology.

John 12.41 might seem an exception to this. John writes of Isaiah: 'Isaiah said this because he saw his glory and spoke of him.' The reference must be to Isaiah's vision in the temple, since Isa. 6.10 has just been quoted. Does John then claim that Isaiah saw *Jesus* in the temple? If we follow the grammar of the sentence we must say Yes, since the ultimate subject of 'him' is 'Jesus' in verse 36. But the word 'Lord' in the quotation from Isa. 6.10 has come in between, and I believe John is not here committing himself to so bizarre a doctrine. It was the pre-existent Lord whom Isaiah saw. He is identical with the Word, who later became incarnate in Jesus.

There is one other passage to which we may refer as we try to decide the relationship of Jesus to the Word in the Fourth Gospel. It is John 10.31–36. We have here the rather mysterious quotation of Psalm 82.6 on the lips of Jesus. I believe that when we look at contemporary exegesis of this psalm we must conclude that John regards it as having been uttered by the pre-existent Word.[30] In that case the phrase in 10.35: 'if he called them gods to whom the word of God came' should be printed 'to whom the Word of God came', and John is therefore referring to the activity of the pre-existent Word, not the pre-existent Jesus, in Israel's history.

It is, therefore, not unreasonable to conclude that John did not see the need to suppose that Jesus Christ had existed as a person before the incarnation. The divine Word or Son or Only-begotten had always existed as a distinction within the godhead. He was capable on occasion of appearing in the form of man during Israel's history, and when the Word became flesh he lived in this world for thirty odd years, as Jesus

Christ. The exact nature of the relation between the Word and Jesus in the Fourth Gospel we cannot know for certain. What is certain is that the picture of Jesus in this gospel eventually gave rise to the doctrine of the hypostatic union between the Logos and his human nature. It seemed probable that this development did do justice to John's intention and that John did envisage something like what either the Alexandrian or the Antiochene versions of the church's traditional christology imply, i.e. that behind the appearance of Jesus there was the person of the divine Word. But I do not see that this in any way involved the consequence that Jesus pre-existed as a person, as both Karl Barth and C. F. D. Moule maintain.

In the Fourth Gospel we do have some evidence about the humanity of the Lord after his resurrection, though it is not easy to interpret. Scholars are not agreed as to the significance of the words: 'Do not hold me, for I have not yet ascended to the Father' in 20.17. But one can claim good authority for the interpretation that the sentence is intended to commend the knowledge of Jesus which was available to any faithful Christian as opposed to too much reliance on the demonstrative power of the resurrection appearances.[31] If so, it is in line with what are probably Jesus' last recorded words in the body of the gospel: 'Blessed are those who have not seen and yet believe' (20.29). This would suggest that John did not lay great store by the actual risen body of the Lord: the ascended state, when the Lord would be available to all believers, is what really matters. It is true that much of the 'information' about the Lord's risen body which caused so much discussion among later theologians comes from the account of the resurrection appearances in the Fourth Gospel. That body could pass through closed doors, could be touched, preserved the marks of the wounds, was perhaps capable of digesting food (21.12). But it is doubtful whether John (or his continuator in chapter 21) was concerned to give us authentic information about the nature of the risen body. These details seem mainly intended to convince the disciples that he really had risen.

There are also, of course, the references in chapter 6 to eating Christ's flesh and drinking his blood. These must have a eucharistic significance. But we are not justified in assuming that by these words John intended to suggest a direct connection, still less identification, between the risen body that Mary clasped and Thomas was invited to touch, and the eucharistic elements. The connection must be what Martelet rightly calls 'symbolic'. I conclude therefore that there is no strong evidence in the Fourth Gospel for a doctrine of a 'glorified humanity' or for a physical body located somewhere in heaven. The divine Word had indeed become flesh in Jesus Christ. But the risen and ascended Lord had no further need for this physical flesh, and a relationship of faith between the believer and the Word of the Father now known in the image of Jesus Christ is commended by the evangelist.

Before I draw the two positive conclusions which emerge from this long and complicated discussion of the pre-existence doctrine, I ought to make it clear why I consider it impossible, in the light of modern knowledge, to defend the concept which we have found both in Karl Barth and C. F. D. Moule of a pre-existent person called Jesus who became incarnate during thirty years in the time of the early Roman Empire, retaining apparently a knowledge of his divine nature and a memory of his pre-incarnate state. My reasons are as follows:

(a) This particular doctrine is, I believe, a combination of several traditions in the New Testament: as we have seen, Paul thought of the heavenly man Jesus appearing in Israel's history and then becoming incarnate. John represents the Logos, enfleshed in Jesus, as remembering his pre-incarnate state and being aware of his divine status. We have no evidence at all as to whether Paul thought of Jesus as aware of his divinity, etc. during the days of his flesh. Thus, though this doctrine can appeal to scriptural evidence, it cannot point to any one writer in the New Testament who certainly combines these two views.

(b) The notion of the pre-existent Son or Word appearing in Israel's history has strong scriptural support, but it must be incredible to us today because of our modern attitude towards scripture. Most of the incidents in which the New Testament writers trace the activity of the pre-incarnate Word we now know to be legend, not history. This applies to the appearance of the angel at the oaks of Mamre; Jacob wrestling with an angel; Moses encountering God in the burning bush; the pillar of cloud in the wilderness; Moses' encounter with God in the tabernacle. Only when we come to the visions of Isaiah and Ezekiel do we encounter historical narrative. The essential feature of legendary narrative is that we cannot press the details; we can be confident at the most of the vaguest outlines of history enshrined in legend. But as far as the alleged appearances of the pre-existent Christ are concerned it is the details that are important. There can be no point in maintaining that it was really the pre-existing Christ who appeared to Jacob in his dream at Bethel if the whole story was originally an aetiological cult legend.

(c) The concept of the Word of God, God in his mode of being as related to his creatures, is perfectly comprehensible and worthy of consideration today. And I believe that by far the best account of how God and man were united in the historical Jesus is to say that he was fully indwelt by the Word of God. But to say, as both Barth and Moule wish to do, that a pre-existent person called Jesus became incarnate, verges on myth rather than theology. We know why Paul had to express himself that way, but this does not mean that we are justified in doing so. As for the doctrine of the 'heavenly man' in Paul, and the suggestion in Barth that Jesus has always been man from eternity, the correlate in modern terms to this is the statement that obedient human-ity (which means an obedient human being) is the supremely appro-priate and effective means for the revelation of the character of the divine Word. We can very properly extend this by saying that the long evolution of *homo sapiens* was part of God's design to reveal himself fully when the time should come.

(d) Finally, there is the claim, made by Barth and not disclaimed by Moule (one gains the impression that he would like to believe it if only the evidence were sufficient), that a pre-existent divine person called Jesus became incarnate, but still retained an awareness of his divine status and a memory of his pre-incarnate state. This, I believe, cannot be believed by many educated Christians today for three very sound reasons. First, the historical evidence that in fact Jesus of Nazareth was conscious of his divinity and remembered his pre-incarnate state is totally insufficient. Practically all the evidence for it comes from the Fourth Gospel, and critical study of that gospel makes it impossible to believe that it is retailing reliable historical information in those pass-ages where Jesus is represented in this light. Admittedly this fact has not yet percolated to the consciousness of a great many educated Christians who might well be expected to have realized it by now. For example, Edward Schillebeeckx's inquisitors can hardly have realized it. And I have recently read a very well-commended and care-fully presented account of Anglicanism whose author, formerly dean of an Anglican Cathedral and now a bishop, treats the Fourth Gospel throughout his work as a piece of entirely reliable reportage.[32] But the fact remains that the Fourth Gospel cannot be accepted as presenting a historically reliable picture of Jesus. Hence we do not believe in a Jesus aware of his own divinity primarily because there is no good evidence that he was.

The second reason why we cannot accept a Jesus aware of his own divinity and conscious of pre-incarnate experience is that it casts doubt on the reality of the incarnation. The great appeal of Christianity has always been that in Jesus Christ God came nearer to us men than ever before. A Jesus who knew he was God is not a Jesus who is one of us. For all his sharing in our history, he would have had an advantage over us which none of us could hope to emulate. He could not have lived by faith, as large parts of the New Testament, including Paul, Mark, and Luke and Hebrews, say he did. The whole point of the doctrine of the incarnation is that in Jesus God accepted the vulnerability of human destiny. An omniscient Jesus, aware of his divinity and conscious of pre-existence, has already forearmed himself against some of the most painful experiences to which we are subject precisely because we are human. The third reason can be expressed very simply: a pre-existent person called Jesus who becomes incarnate while retaining a memory of his pre-incarnate state, is myth, not history or theology. He belongs to the same category as Krishna or Dionysius.

I hope by this time to have clarified the significance of the New Testament attribution of pre-existence to Jesus or to the Logos. I must now specify the two elements in this tradition which we can retain today in our reconstruction of christology. The first need not detain us long; it is the Logos doctrine. I have already made clear what sort of a Logos doctrine I believe to be necessary. It seems to me that if one is to bring the career of Jesus into integral connection with the being and action of God, one has to accept some doctrine of distinctions within the godhead, which is what a Logos doctrine is. As we have seen, at one stage very early in its existence the Christian church appeared to be proclaiming a doctrine of two gods, God the Father, and Jesus Christ. This intellectually impossible position was averted by the adoption of a Logos doctrine. The author of Colossians has done this in all but name. John does it quite consciously. Very early in the second century Ignatius of Antioch has a Logos doctrine. It is important that we emphasize that it is *a* Logos doctrine that is needed, because we should not regard ourselves as necessarily committed to the Logos doctrine which any one early Christian theologian puts forward. As we have seen, there are grave difficulties about some aspects of John's Logos doctrine: as he expounds it, it runs too close to safeguarding a theophany rather than an incarnation. The same might be said for Ignatius' Logos doctrine: 'God being manifested in human form' is not an altogether satisfactory way of expressing it.[33] There is no reason to believe that John's Logos doctrine was the only one in the early church: Ignatius' tradition may well be independent of John's, and of course that which we find in Colossians is quite independent also.

The other element which we can usefully employ is Paul's conception of the pre-existent Christ as being God manifested in the form or image of man. Paul, we have seen, probably worked this out for himself in order to relate the revelation in Christ to the theophanies of the Old Testament. But we wish to employ it as a useful analogy for the form of Jesus Christ in the post-resurrection period. In Paul's thought the pre-existent Christ was only man in a 'heavenly' ideal sense. He did not possess the limitations of humanity. He could therefore appear at various points in Israel's history in the form of man because that, in fact, is the form which God, when he chose to reveal his character fully, chose to adopt. But he could still be related as God to the faithful in Israel. He did not have the problems entailed by a physical body.

This can be applied, *mutatis mutandis*, to our understanding of the relation of the risen Jesus Christ to God the Word, and to believers. The individual Jesus of Nazareth, raised from the dead by the power of God, now exists in the eternal dimension, related no doubt to the departed saints in a mode which we cannot possibly fathom. But since the divine Word, God in his mode of being as related to this creation, chose to indwell Jesus Christ in order to reveal himself fully and finally to men, we can claim that Christian believers now know God in the form or image of Jesus Christ. Jesus Christ represents to us the character of God. God the Word has chosen that we should know him as he was in Jesus Christ. We have consistently maintained throughout this work and in *Grace and Truth* that Jesus is the true reflection or reproduction on a human scale of God's character. God is personal and can only be known to us in a person-to-person encounter. Not that we would confine God to the category of person, but we must say that he is known to us as not less than personal. Since the resurrection we know him as manifested in the person of Jesus Christ. Jesus Christ is therefore for us permanently the image of the invisible God.

When Christians worship God, they do not worship Jesus. They worship God-in-Christ. But God-in-Christ is the manifestation of the eternal Word. We can if we like substitute the term 'Son' and say that God-in-Christ is the eternal Son. Indeed the use of 'Son' for the Second Person of the Trinity is so deeply entrenched in biblical and traditional vocabulary that it would be absurd to try to dispense with it. I have, however, used the term 'Word' instead as a general rule because the indiscriminate use of the term 'Son' always tends towards an *identification* of Jesus with the eternal Son, precisely what we have tried to avoid in our reconstructed christology. I suppose if one wished to distinguish this christology from the traditional account of Christ one might say that whereas according to the traditional account Christians worship God identified with Christ, according to this christology we worship God known in Christ. In each case Christ is at the centre of our worship.

Does this christology depreciate the incarnation? Traditional theologians have been accustomed to claim that ever since the incarnation mankind is integrally related to God: a new intimate relationship between God and man has been instituted. It seems to me that when this claim is investigated it runs out into meaninglessness. In so far as God the Son in traditional christology is still man his humanity can have no connection with Christians on earth, since it must be finite, or it would not be humanity. The attempt to 'deify' it as the Eastern Orthodox tradition does, and as Westcott and Swete implicitly do, leads either to meaninglessness or to a humanity that has been completely dissolved in divinity. My reconstruction of christology on the other hand can say with perfect intelligibility that God the Word is now related to the faithful in the form or image of Jesus Christ, without any of those embarrassing problems which arise when one tries to retain Jesus' humanity attached to the Word in some way or other.

Nor does this approach to christology depreciate or truncate the effect of the incarnation in such a way as to render it merely an incident in the dealings of God with men. Because of the incarnation God is now and for ever fully revealed in the image of Jesus Christ. A new epoch in the relation between God and men did begin with the coming of Jesus, both because he is now fully revealed as he was not before, and because it is now a universal revelation as it was not before. We can never dispense with the image of Jesus Christ. He is the permanent mode in which God the Word is known to us. What we have dispensed with is the embarrassment of having to attach a human nature permanently to God and to explain how that which must be finite can perform a function which only the infinite God can perform. According to this christology, when Christians say that they worship the Lord Jesus Christ, they mean that they worship God the Word, known in the form of Jesus Christ.

For the rest of this book we must occupy ourselves in finding further analogies, biblical and otherwise, that may illuminate this account of the risen Christ, and in attempting to clarify what is meant by the heavenly intercession of Christ.

Five

Models and Objections

In the last chapter I claimed that the New Testament doctrine of the pre-existent Christ could serve as a useful analogy for the status of the risen Christ in our belief today. But this reassessment of the rôle of Christ needs more than an analogy. We would be helped if we could find models in scripture or elsewhere that would enable us to realize that we are not being asked to accept some completely unheard of approach. This chapter attempts to provide such models.

First, however, and by way of transition, it will be convenient to refer to a recent article by the Rev. Keith Ward, Dean of Trinity Hall, Cambridge.[1] We take note of it because the author expresses very clearly the philosophical difficulties involved in claiming that the humanity of Jesus Christ is available to all the faithful since his resurrection, and because he comes to tentative conclusions which are very like those which we defend in this work.

He is actually commenting on the same article by Brian Hebblethwaite, 'Incarnation – The Essence of Christianity?', which was discussed in Chapter 1.[2] He begins by doubting the claim which Hebblethwaite says is implicit in the traditional christology, that we can have a direct personal encounter with God because we meet him in Jesus Christ. We can only have such an encounter if we meet a person. But Jesus died nearly two thousand years ago. He next considers the answer to this objection that defenders of traditional christology would make: Jesus is not dead, they would say, but rose again and 'in his glorified but still human body, he sits in heaven at God's right hand'. Ward still asks: 'Can I have a face to face encounter with a glorified heavenly body?' He concludes that this is not possible and that even the modification that it is Jesus' mind which we meet will not hold water. It means that we encounter 'a being who can be simultaneously related in the same way to thousands of other persons on earth'. And he asks: 'Is this any longer a human being?'

He then passes on to another possible argument of the defenders of traditional christology: 'Jesus shows what God is ... without him, God would remain the unknown transcendent. We do have a sense of direct personal encounter with God; and we do have it because of Jesus. We say that Jesus expressed truly what God is, so it is proper to conceive God by thinking of the man Jesus.' Ward replies in effect that we can have all this (and note how close it is to my suggestion of Jesus Christ as the image of God) without requiring the doctrine that God became man in Jesus Christ. He backs this up with a number of convincing arguments, one of which we may reproduce: 'it would never do to point to the historical Jesus and say "There is God" *tout court*'. In fact however this is what a great deal of popular preaching and devotion does.

Ward next tackles another argument put forward by Hebblethwaite in his article, to the effect that in the incarnation God 'bore the brunt of human suffering himself', and this claim depends entirely on the traditional doctrine of hypostatic union. Ward replies first that the suffering of one man can hardly be described as bearing the evil of the whole world, and secondly that in any case the traditional doctrine of the incarnation did not really permit God to suffer at all. The fathers always defended the impassibility of God. If Hebblethwaite wants a theology that allows God to suffer, he will have to modify traditional christology.

Hebblethwaite's final argument is 'if God might have become man, but did not, then the reduced claims for what God has done in Christ fail to satisfy'. Ward schematizes this argument thus: 'if x is logically possible; and if we think it better than y, then x', and points out that this could justify all sorts of absurd claims about what God must have done, starting with the Assumption of the Blessed Virgin Mary. And he very rightly concludes: 'If we want to know whether God became man, in the "two natures, one person" sense, we have to examine the evidence.'

At the end of his article Keith Ward protests against the particular dilemma which Brian Hebblethwaite has proposed: 'Either Jesus is a clever, inspired man or he is God'. He claims that there are other ways of expressing the doctrine of the incarnation: 'Incarnation might not be the subsumption of one substantial nature by another but the clear manifestation of transcendence at one point in history which draws together and gives particular expression to its partially hidden manifestations at all times and places.' This is only a mere hint of a doctrine, he adds, but 'it may give a glimpse of a doctrine which will be incarnationalist in every sense Hebblethwaite desires', but will not give us the misleading dichotomy: 'Jesus was either an inspired man or a totally unique species of being, the eternal Logos with a human mind and body. Perhaps he was a man in whom the glory of God was manifested fully, and through whom God will bring to himself all who will respond.'

This brief article, it seems to me, admirably sums up precisely the difficulties inherent in the traditional account of the risen Jesus which was considered in Chapter 2, and points to the sort of alternative approach which I am outlining in the present work. Particularly interesting is the reference to the concept of the suffering God, since this is very much the topic to be examined in the next chapter. With this beginning I can now go on in this chapter to elaborate this doctrine of the risen Christ by proposing some models that may help us. This will involve us in the very necessary task of considering the two other areas in which the phrase 'the body of Christ' is used in the New Testament, that is, the area of the church and of the eucharist. Finally we must face a number of objections that could be made against the approach I propose. This, in its turn, will require some discussion of the late Professor G. W. H. Lampe's last book, *God as Spirit*.[3]

I have two models to put forward, both drawn from the tradition of Judaism. The first is this: we can think of the risen Christ in terms analogous to the part which the Torah plays in Judaism. In Judaism it is God's covenant with Israel that is the permanently uniting bond. God has chosen Israel out of all the peoples of the world to be his special people. He has given them the Torah as a pledge of his care for them. They are to observe the Torah by way of responding to his love in choosing them and the Torah is at the same time the means by which they remain within his covenant. It is at one and the same time the revelation of the sort of person God is and the revelation of the sort of people he wants Israel to be. Of course I am now thinking in terms of orthodox Judaism. I am not raising the question of how the Torah came to be regarded in this way or whether this is the true meaning of the Old Testament. Such questions are not relevant to our purpose here.

May we not regard the relation of Jesus Christ to Christians in this way also? We too are covenant partners with God. At the Last Supper Jesus referred to the new covenant in his blood, and Hebrews calls him the mediator of a new covenant (8.6; 9.15; 12.24). He is therefore the pledge to us of God's election. Just as when the old covenant was made between God and Israel on Sinai the Torah was given as its sign and pledge, so is Jesus given as the sign and pledge of the new covenant. It is true that Paul uses this word 'pledge' not of Christ but of the Spirit (II Cor. 1.22; 5.5 and cf. Eph. 1.14), but in his thought the Spirit was the means by which we know the risen Christ, and, as I shall be noting in Chapter 7, he did not always clearly distinguish between the risen Christ and the Spirit. Similarly Jesus Christ is to us the revelation of God's character and at the same time the revelation of what God wishes humanity to be. This is why Paul can call him both the *eikōn* of God and the *eikōn* of man.

When we make the comparison of Jesus Christ in Christianity with the Torah in Judaism we may also claim that Christ fulfils his function better than the Torah because he is a person not a code, and also because he is a universal model, not one confined to one people or tradition. This first reason perhaps requires some explanation. Might it not be objected that the doctrine of the risen Christ I am expounding precisely excludes the possibility that Christians can encounter the person of Jesus Christ? This is true if by 'the person of Jesus Christ' is meant the human personality of Jesus of Nazareth. As Keith Ward has so ably demonstrated, it is philosophically impossible to defend the statement that Christians by faith know the personality of Jesus of Nazareth. But this does not mean that we do not know God the Word personally. We do, in the sense in which Christians have always claimed that they knew God as personal. What we insist is that since the incarnation he is known to Christians in the form of Jesus Christ. In order to make this claim we do not have to maintain that the human personality of Jesus is available to us.

We now take up the second reason: God is capable of being known in the form or image of Jesus Christ not just by Israel, but by all men. When we apply this to Jesus as model for what God wishes us to be, we can say that in Jesus Christ we have the God-given model for the new humanity. His human nature as such is permanently necessary for us as a model or example, but, so far, only to the extent of being a symbol or picture. So far as we have considered it up to this point, it could be no more than a historical reminiscence.

Perhaps this can be taken further: I have argued that in the human life of Jesus God's character was manifested not accidentally but necessarily. The teaching, service, suffering and death of Jesus Christ were the unique, necessary and indispensible method by which the true character of God could be manifested to us men. The Word of God, being by definition God in his relation to his creatures and supremely to man, is always to be known in the humanity of Christ. The cross is always the hall-mark of God in his dealings with us. Our way of being 'in' God the Word, as he wills it, is through the pattern of the life of Jesus Christ: we are called to serve, to bear the cross, to die, to rise again – all very much according to Paul's doctrine of life 'in Christ'. The Word is present to us in the mode of Christ, known to us in the image of Christ. The Word's Christness is perfectly fitted to our humanity.

Thus the community of the church is the means by which the human nature of Christ (which is ontologically in the eternal dimension and not available to us) is still permanently relevant now. This is why Paul elaborated his difficult but necessary doctrine of the church as the body of Christ, instead of doing as subsequent Christian theologians did and trying to maintain a doctrine of a 'glorified humanity'. In his article on the body of Christ already mentioned,[4] Eduard Schweizer has described the church in Paul's thought as 'Christ's space' (*das Raum Christi*). The church is the space in which we begin here on earth the process whereby hereafter we attain full membership of Christ's body. Paul's doctrine of the church (as of everything else) is eschatological. It is intended to explain how we can live now so as ultimately to inherit those 'spiritual bodies' which will enable us to have full fellowship with Christ, who is already fully in the realm of the Spirit as we are not. We can well understand why the author of Ephesians has slightly modified this doctrine, perhaps under the conviction that the parousia is not to be expected nearly as soon as Paul imagined. In Ephesians the church is a dynamic organism, something that is growing and into which the individual can grow. See especially Ephesians 4.1–16. Thus full union between redeemed humanity and the risen Christ is only to be expected at the *eschaton*, not in this life, where we have to be content with a 'pledge' of a 'first-fruits'. Significantly enough, this latter word is applied by Paul both to the Spirit and to Christ (see Rom. 8.23; I Cor. 15.20, 23). It is relevant to observe in this connection that when Paul is speaking of the risen Christ, or of Christians who shall be risen hereafter, he prefers the language of spirit. Even that paradoxical phrase 'spiritual bodies' is only used because of a complete lack of alternative vocabulary. He uses the term 'bodies' because he wants to retain our human personality, our finiteness even in the hereafter. But he uses the adjective 'spiritual' and claims that Christ is now a 'living spirit' (I Cor. 15.45), because the relationship between Christ and Christians must not be thought of in physical, spatial terms. Christ's own humanity is known to us in this life only in the humanity of the members of the church in so far as they reproduce the pattern of his life. The model of the Torah in Judaism has therefore helped us to bridge the gap between the risen Christ and the church viewed as his body. It reminds us that Jesus Christ is at one and the same time the revelation of God and the pattern for humanity. We can have a doctrine of the church as the body of Christ without involving ourselves in the impossible task of identifying that body with either the body that was crucified or the 'glorified humanity' of the risen Lord.

Paul also uses the phrase 'the Lord's body' of the eucharist, and in any case we have the tradition of the institution of the eucharist recorded in the New Testament, as well as the undeniably eucharistic passages in the Fourth Gospel. How is this to be related to the risen Christ? We have already observed in Chapter 2 that traditional Christian theology has always tried to establish a link between the Lord's body in the eucharist, his risen body, and the body crucified for us. Many theologians have claimed that all three bodies are 'identical'. Even Martelet shows a desire to do this.[5] What are we to make of this?

Perhaps we should begin by stepping back and trying to see the eucharist in perspective. Nearly all traditions in Christianity are now agreed in understanding the eucharist as being primarily a thanksgiving for God's acts of salvation in Christ, a thanksgiving in which our own Christian service (that 'spiritual worship' of which Paul writes in

Romans 12.1) is focussed and concentrated, so that our giving of ourselves to God in Christ, which is the essence of the Christian's way of
life, is made explicit and consciously associated with Christ's offering
of himself to the Father. Thus the two great controversies concerning
the eucharist which troubled the theologians of the Reformation period
have very largely been resolved, or are at least in process of being
resolved. There is no need to maintain that the eucharist is a repetition
of Christ's sacrifice, but, since self-offering to God is of the essence of
the Christian life, Christ's sacrifice cannot be omitted from the eucharist. And secondly, we need not be too much concerned about the mode
of Christ's presence in the bread and the wine, because the eucharist
does not mean essentially the making sacred of bread and wine. The
bread and the wine are the means by which the eucharistic action is
carried out, but they are not, as 'consecrated elements', the sole
cynosure of the eucharist. The essence of the eucharist consists in
giving thanks and partaking in the bread and the wine.

It follows, therefore, that we should not insist on a special sort of
'eucharistic presence' of God in Christ, different from the way in which
he is present to the believer on all other occasions. The eucharist is the
focussing in one conscious, churchly action of the presence of God in
Christ which is always available to the believer. In just the same way,
we should not talk about 'eucharistic grace' as if it was a special brand
of grace, different from grace as given on other occasions. God is the
great giver, and his grace is always the same. In the eucharist that grace
is covenanted, focussed, to be relied on if we have faith. It is not a
different sort of grace. Grace is not an impersonal force like electricity.
It is God's personal presence. He has promised us his presence in the
form of Christ at the eucharist. If we have faith we can encounter him
there in the form of Christ.

R. H. Gundry has recently published a valuable study of Paul's use
of the phrase 'body of Christ' in which he concludes that the eucharist
in its original institution at the Last Supper was intended to denote the
sacrifice of the victim:[6] the bread represents the body broken, the wine
the blood shed. In other words, the eucharist is par excellence the
sacrament of the self-giving of God. In it God's nature as self-giving
is revealed, represented, re-experienced. This revelation is indissolubly
connected with the historical Jesus. When, therefore, we say that Christ
is present at the eucharist, we mean that God the Word is present in

that mode whereby his true nature becomes most perspicuous, the mode of self-giving. But that mode *is* Jesus Christ, it is the mode or pattern into which God has chosen to fit in order to speak to us most effectively and in order that we may know him best. This is not to say that he is present to us in each eucharist exactly as he was present to the disciples in the upper room, but that he is present sacramentally in the image of Jesus Christ. God is known to us in Christ in exactly the same sense as that in which we partake of Christ's body and blood, i.e. sacramentally, mystically, not physically, corporeally or sensibly.[7]

We must try to avoid the traditional static view of the eucharist. It is nothing if not a dynamic action. In it we are neither trying to manipulate God, nor are we hoping to produce the body and blood of Christ on the altar, so that they can be viewed by the faithful. To quote a recent work on the doctrine of the eucharist: 'Biblical language lends itself neither to the mediaeval tendency to turn metaphors into metaphysics nor to the literalist desire to take them as scientific statements. In speaking of Christ's body and blood as present in the eucharist we are using the highly symbolic, highly equivocal language of imagery, and it is only a matter of common sense to tread carefully and delicately here.'[8] It should be noted that what Jesus singled out for attention at the Last Supper was bread and wine, associating them with his body and blood. In the course of Christian history an unbalanced emphasis has been laid on the word 'body'. The blood, which claims equal place in our attention, has too often been ignored. *The* problem of the eucharist has therefore usually taken the form of asking: how does Christ's body appear in the eucharist? Perhaps this is the wrong question to ask, and that is why the answers have been so unsatisfactory. 'Why should we want to hold in our hands or our mouths Christ's body which is admitted by all not to be present in any spatial way nor in any way apprehensible by the senses? The symbolism of bread/wine corresponding to body/blood is not of a reduplication of Christ for us but of our involvement in his redeeming self-giving.'

If we return to the thought of Christ's body and his blood being given for us, we find a more satisfactory line of thought to pursue. These two together represent the life of Jesus as given for us. They are the gift of life in God-in-Christ. They are the gifts of God in the church and for the church, and are therefore only available for faith. Hence we must describe what happens in the eucharist as a mystery not as a miracle. This is entirely in line with the thinking of the Fathers of the church and particularly with the eucharistic doctrine of the Eastern Orthodox traditions. And this means that at the eucharist we are in the world of the Holy Spirit. 'The Holy Spirit is Lord of time, and is also the pledge of our resurrection and the arrival and presence in our midst of heaven. It is peculiarly appropriate to recall that it is only because we are in the Holy Spirit that the eucharist is not an empty formula, a piece of play-acting.'

In *The Risen Christ and the Eucharistic World*, Martelet has an interesting account of the way in which the doctrine of the eucharist fell into the hands of the metaphysicians in the mediaeval church in the West. He writes: 'Thus ... in order to preserve more surely the Corpus Christi they abandoned the concept of body in favour of the concept of substance.'[9] He goes on to show how the defenders of transubstantiation were suspicious of the use of the word 'spiritual' in connection with the mode of Christ's presence in the eucharistic elements, because they thought it meant 'incorporeal', and they thus deprived themselves of the use of the one scriptural word they most needed. They went on to elaborate an explanation of transubstantiation that was expressly designed to exclude a crude literalistic understanding of the eucharistic presence. But it has the disadvantage that it was framed in Aristotelian categories that do not make sense today.

Martelet puts plenty of emphasis on the eucharist as the revelation of God in Christ: 'The Eucharist is the sacramental emergence of the mystery'.[10] He interprets 'transubstantiation' in terms of 'transignification' or 'transfinalization' (the eucharistic elements show what creation is intended by God to be).[11] Christ's risen body which, he claims, is present in the eucharist, he wishes to regard in terms of relation rather than as a thing.[12] The link between physical body and eucharistic body is to be spiritual body, what he calls an identity of person but not of states.[13] This seems to me to be very much what I am arguing for: we encounter the person of Christ at the eucharist because Christ is the image of the divine Word, and he always encounters us personally. Martelet also seems to take the same view about the link between the eucharist and the church: it lies in the new humanity. He writes that in his resurrection the new Adam inaugurated not only the new humanity but also the new nature and in the eucharist we gain the first-fruits of this.[14] I entirely agree that there is this eschatological aspect of the eucharist. It is what Charles Wesley calls it, 'the antepast of heaven'. In the hereafter we may hope to share fully in the new humanity in the body of the risen Christ. In this life we may begin to do so by virtue of our relationship to God-in-Christ in the Spirit. God-in-Christ is the Word known in the image of Jesus Christ. Lastly we may note that Martelet also puts the same emphasis as I do on the element of God's self-giving in the eucharist. He writes: 'Christ is much less in the bread and the wine than the bread and the wine are in him. . . . He is present under the stigmata of his absence and the kenosis of his glory.'[15] In other words, the eucharist, though it is the memorial of the whole of God's saving action towards mankind, finds its climax and burning centre in the cross of Jesus Christ, for Paul as for John the very moment where the character of God is more clearly revealed to the eyes of faith than anywhere else. But it is of course a cross that is not artificially isolated and divorced from the resurrection, as it is far too much in Cranmer's eucharistic liturgy of 1552.[16]

It is only when Martelet writes of an 'identity' between the physical body crucified and risen on the one hand and the body we encounter in the eucharist on the other that I cannot agree with him.[17] This is perhaps because he begins from what I regard as an untenable position about the risen body of Christ. But when he comes to give his account of how Christ is present in the eucharist he seems to me to hold to an admirable 'relational' theology. Despite his belief that he has maintained some sort of identity between the physical, historical body of Jesus and the eucharistic elements, it seems to me that he has, in effect, abandoned any attempt to bring the humanity of Christ into the eucharistic presence in any but a symbolic way. This is very much the mode in which I believe we ought to think of it.

I have neither the space here, nor ability to consider the eucharistic doctrine of the Eastern Orthodox tradition, though no doubt it has much to teach us. However, one point may be made. Martelet writes that according to John of Damascus 'the post-consecratory epiclesis . . . causes the sensible elements which before were only figures, to pass into the reality, properly so-called, of the body of Christ'.[18] This tendency to abandon the language of mysticism for that of realism was reinforced by the experience of the Iconoclastic controversy which continued after the time of John of Damascus. At the Iconoclast Council of 754 it was declared that the only admissible symbol of Christ is the eucharist. The Iconodules replied that the eucharist was not symbol but reality. The eucharist is Christ's risen body penetrated by the divine energies.[19] This seems to me to be attempting to storm heaven: what is done in the eucharist is done symbolically, sacramentally, mystically, not corporeally, sensibly or literally. The Iconoclast argument seems to me to be valid: there is a sense in which the eucharist is a representation of Christ. But this does not mean that it is unreal, ineffective, or play-acting. As long as we are in the flesh we can only know God by faith and express our knowledge in symbols. Hereafter it will be different. But faith is not speculation: we do know him. And images are not mere expressions of our hopes: they really do convey God in Christ.

Thus I hope to have shown that the approach to the doctrine of the risen Christ put forward in this work, though it excludes the possibility of Christ's human personality encountering us in the eucharist, does, nevertheless, give a meaning to the conception of the body of Christ in the eucharist which is faithful to the New Testament witness and enables us to claim sincerely that those who have faith do meet God in Christ at the table of the Lord.

The model of the Torah in Judaism has taken us far afield, but it has provided us with something of a bridge between the historical Jesus and the use of 'body' for the risen body of Jesus, for the church, and for the consecrated elements in the eucharist. Our second model is taken from the Old Testament itself; it is the model of the Name of God. According to the third chapter of the Book of Exodus, when God appeared to Moses in the burning bush in order to announce his intention of freeing the Israelites from slavery in Egypt, he, at the same time, announced his new name, Yahweh. Other traditions in the Old Testament have other accounts, it is true, but this is certainly the story as given by one early and very influential tradition. The new Name is connected with the act of redemption, though it does not etymologically have any overtone of redemption attached to it. Centuries later rabbinic tradition distinguished between *'elōhīm* ('God') and *Adonai* ('Lord'), the form in which 'Yahweh' was invariably read by those reading the scriptures in public. Some Rabbis held that *'elōhīm* indicated God's attribute of justice, and *Adonai* his attribute of mercy.[20] Frequently in the Old Testament also God identifies himself as the God of Abraham, of Isaac, and of Jacob. We think of Blaise Pascal's great conversion experience, which he tries to describe with the words 'the God of Abraham, of Isaac, and of Jacob and not the God of the scientists'. In other words, he had come to know the living God who reveals himself by means of what he does, as contrasted with the Deist conception of a God of abstract qualities.

Apply this to God known in Jesus Christ. The supreme act of salvation is signalled by God identifying himself with Jesus Christ, as he identified himself with Abraham, with Isaac, with Jacob, with Moses. He identified himself not by declaring 'I am Abraham', etc. but by showing his character in his dealings with these individuals. How much more has he shown himself to be the God of Jesus Christ, whose name means 'Anointed Saviour'! There are several places in the New Testament where 'Christ' really means 'anointed one' and one or two where 'Jesus' means 'Saviour', e.g. Matthew 1.21. I have sometimes wondered whether Paul may not have this in mind on the two occasions on which he quotes Isaiah 45.23: 'To me every knee shall bow, every tongue shall swear' (see Rom. 14.11; Phil. 2.11). In the second passage he adds 'every tongue shall swear that Jesus Christ is Lord'. Only two verses earlier, in Isaiah 45.21 he would have read:

> Who told this long ago?
> Who declared it of old?
> Was it not I, the Lord?
> And there is no god besides me,
> A righteous God and a Saviour.

In 'Jesus Christ is Lord' we have both 'Lord' and 'Saviour'. Does Paul believe that in this passage of Isaiah the prophet is hinting at the new name of God 'Jesus the Saviour'?

When I was teaching in a theological college in South India and I learned Telugu, one of the four languages of the southern part of the sub-continent, I was dismayed to find that the earliest missionaries in the last century had not hesitated to transliterate the Name of God in the Old Testament, the Tetragrammaton, and to transliterate it in the popular but incorrect form 'Jehovah'. The consequence was that some of the hymns which Telugu Christians had composed for use in worship actually employed 'Jehovah' indiscriminately to refer to God the Father. One very popular hymn began 'Jehovah is my shepherd'. This is as shocking as the translation of John 1.1 perpetrated by a popular modern

version of the Bible: 'In the beginning was Christ'. God only needs a
name in order to distinguish him from others in the same category.
Once you have realized (as Israel did as early as the time of the exile)
that there is only one God, you do not need a name for him – and, in
fact, after the exile Israel ceased to use his name freely.

But the sort of naming that I have in mind is not like that. It is a
naming in order to manifest God's character, not in order to distinguish
him from other gods. We might associate God's calling himself the
God of Abraham with the use of the term 'the word of God' in the Old
Testament. God utters his word at any point where he does something
significant in history: he utters it at creation. God says 'Fiat Lux' and
the universe comes into existence. At the time of the Assyrian invasion,
Isaiah of Jerusalem claims that God 'has sent his word against Jacob,
and it will light upon Israel' (Isa. 9.8). Jeremiah sees the action of the
word of God in the traumatic events of his day and compares it to fire
and to 'a hammer which breaks the rock in pieces' (Jer. 23.29). Hundreds of years later the author of the Book of Wisdom[21] writes a
brilliant description of the Word of God like 'a stern warrior carrying
the sharp sword of (God's) authentic command' as he executes God's
judgment upon the first-born in Egypt (Wisdom 18.15–16). The word
of God always means God's self-expressiveness, his self-revelation in
the events of history. We learn who God is from what he does and this
self-revealed character is expressed both by God associating himself
with various persons in history and by the use of the periphrasis 'the
word of God'.

The risen Christ is then the eternal self-revelation and self-expressiveness of God. Since he has supremely made himself known in a man,
Jesus Christ, he cannot go back on that. The word remains uttered in
Christ, so finally, in fact, that we must say that the Word has uttered
himself in Christ. We will always know God best as uttered in Jesus
Christ – better still, say with Tillich 'in Jesus as the Christ', for this
reminds us of the whole career of Jesus. This does not mean that
'humanity reigns on the throne of the universe', a meaningless piece of
rhetoric, but that, in the actual experience of Christians, God is known
in the image of Christ. How often through the Bible is God characterized as 'the God of . . .'. Hagar, after her vision of the angel in the
wilderness says: 'Thou art a God of seeing' (Gen. 16.13). Perhaps this
can be dismissed or disregarded as belonging to a period which can at

best be described as legendary. Let us then call God a God of the covenant. Better still, describe him as the God of Amos, of Hosea, of Isaiah, of Jeremiah, of the anonymous prophet of the exile, of the brilliant author of the Book of Jonah. This goodly company of the prophets find their culmination in Jesus Christ, who is not God's self-expression just occasionally or verbally, but by means of his entire life, death, and resurrection. In post-exilic times, with the exception of the astonishing little Book of Jonah, the prophetic fellowship dies away, but it is interesting to observe how often leaders in Israel utter on behalf of the people a prayer of penitence which is in itself a summing up of salvation history (see Neh. 9.6–38; Ezra 9.6–15; Dan. 9.4–19). These men made an act of penitence on behalf of Israel in the light of Israel's history. Jesus in a sense acted out this penitence in his death. Piet Schoonenberg notices this tendency in the Old Testament to describe God as 'a God of . . .' and he well quotes Hebrews 11.16: 'Therefore God is not ashamed to be called their God, for he has prepared for them a city.'[22] And Moltmann points out that Paul describes God as 'the God who raises the dead' (II Cor. 1.9) and sees a parallel here to 'the God who led Israel out of Egypt'.[23] Above all we can appeal to the very remarkable usage of Jesus himself according to Mark 12.26. His proof text for the resurrection of the dead is Exodus 3.6: 'I am the God of Abraham and the God of Isaac and the God of Jacob.' God identifies himself by means of those with whom he has had communion. The argument is one from religious experience, and a very strong one for those who have had any religious experience: if God has made himself known to these men during their lifetime, he is not the sort of God to abandon them at death.

Thus the model of the Name of God runs back into the Old Testament and can appeal to the long tradition of God's self-revelation to Israel in history. In Jesus Christ God has named himself afresh and supremely. He has been known as the God of Abraham; he is now known as the God of Jesus Christ. But so much fuller and existential is the revelation in Jesus – it was his very life – that we can say God is known in Jesus. His new name is Jesus Christ. This does not mean that the historical Jesus *was* God, any more than the historical Hosea, or Isaiah, or Jeremiah *was* God. It means that the final and normative revelation of God was in Jesus Christ and that if today we want to know who God is, Christians must point to Jesus Christ, not just as a historical reminiscence, but as the form and image in which we know God now.

I end this chapter by considering three objections to my approach which may arise at this point in the development of the theme. The first two need not detain us very long. This third requires rather more attention:

1. 'You are teaching a doctrine of two Sons; in other words, you are vulnerable to the accusation which Cyril of Alexandria brought against Nestorius, more so, in fact than Nestorius himself was.'

In the sense in which traditional christology understands the matter, I must plead guilty to this charge. But when it is examined, it does not prove to be destructive to a satisfactory christology. We are talking about the relation between God and man in Christ: man's true relationship to God is one of sonship, and that relationship has been supremely and normatively manifested in Christ and is made possible for us in the Spirit (see Rom. 8.15–17). The other partner in the relationship is God, God in his aspect or mode of existence as related to his creatures. We may call this mode God the Son, though I have preferred to use the alternative title 'God the Word' because of the danger of identifying Jesus with God the Son. What the accusation really amounts to is that, according to my approach to the doctrine of the incarnation, God and man are not personally identified. This I freely admit, but I maintain that an adequate christology does not require that they should be. The relationship of indwelling (*kat' eudokian*) seems to me to be adequate as a description. It has a respectable theological ancestry in the Antiochene tradition, and it is the one relationship between God and man which we can know in our own experience.

2. 'In your account of the relation of the risen Jesus to believers you present him as being nothing more than the symbol for God the Word.'

This is the same accusation as Pannenberg brings against Tillich's entire christology. In order to meet it, we must ask what is meant by 'symbol' in this context. During the life of Jesus Christ his perfect humanity was the supreme means of expression of God the Word. If it was a symbol, it was an effective symbol, for a sufficient number of people saw in Jesus the action and purpose of God for the Christian religion to have emerged from the events of that life. Jesus Christ is still the form in which God is known to Christians today. Indeed this term 'form' is a very significant one. Its corresponding word in New Testament Greek is *morphē*. In Phil. 2.6, the pre-existent Christ is described as having existed in the form (*morphē*) of God; and in verse 7 we learn that he was born in the form (*morphē*) of men. In each case *morphē* means 'real form not mere appearance'. The two forms coincide in Jesus Christ and are supremely manifested on the cross. We preach Christ crucified and risen, which is the form in which God the Word is pleased to make himself known to believers. As for the spirit or personality of Jesus himself, he cannot be similarly related to believers in this life at least, but remains in heaven intimately related to the Father through the Son in the communion of saints.

In this connection II Cor. 3.18 may be helpful:

> And we all with unveiled face, beholding[24] the glory of the Lord, are being changed into his likeness from one degree of glory to another; for this comes from the Lord who is the Spirit.

This is a reference to the image (*eikōn*) of the risen Christ serving as a model for Christians in the Spirit. I cannot see that it requires us to believe that the human nature or personality of Jesus is an essential element in their process, whatever Paul himself may have held. And we cannot fail to notice the fact that Paul puts it all in the context of the Spirit. We could if we liked, say that *eikōn* here only means 'a symbol'. But Paul certainly believes that it is an effective symbol, and that without it the redemption which God has carried out through Jesus Christ could not be made available to us. The word for 'are being changed' here is *metamorphoumetha*, etymologically of the same root as *morphē* which we discussed above. Jesus Christ as the *morphē* of God and man enables us to assimilate the same *morphē*.

3. 'Since you have abandoned the theory of hypostatic union, you have no right to use a Logos doctrine, which was only constructed to defend the hypostatic union theory and does not make sense without it.'

We have already argued that a Logos doctrine is not simply the consequence of adopting a theory of hypostatic union. Philo had a doctrine of the Logos without any incarnation theology. Also, something like hypostatic union can be defended by using other terms such as *eikōn*, *sophia* (wisdom), *apaugasma* (Hebrews); *prōtotokos* (Colossians). Hengel would add that *huios* (Son' is another such term used by very early Christians.[25] Indeed it could be plausibly maintained that Logos is not the best term to use in connection with a theory of hypostatic union. 'Son', which has least philosophical overtones, would seem more suitable because of the ease with which it can be adapted to a personal union between God and man – not to mention Jesus' use of 'Abba'. Hence we must be allowed to put forward a Logos doctrine without being accused of having stolen the clothes of traditional christology.

We must, however, pay attention to the late Professor Lampe's last book *God as Spirit*, in which he goes to the other extreme, and puts forward a christology which does not contain a theory of hypostatic union, but which dispenses also with a Logos doctrine and therefore with a doctrine of God as Trinity. We may begin by noticing a few comments he makes in an essay entitled 'The Holy Spirit and the Person of Christ', written a few years earlier.[26] The real objection to the traditional christology, he argues, is that it presents us with a picture of what is, in effect, God incognito; and later he writes: 'the alternative to the (Logos) designation, "Son", involved a constant tendency to project on to the eternal Logos the attributes of human personality'. These are both difficulties with which I wholeheartedly sympathize, as I have shown both in *Grace and Truth* and in the present work. Similarly he has very much the same difficulty with those who claim to 'encounter Jesus Christ' in contemporary experience as we noted in Keith Ward's article with which this chapter began. Would such people, he asks, be content to say that they know God 'according to the pattern of Jesus Christ' or would they insist on saying 'Jesus of Nazareth, the man fully possessed by the Spirit, and thus united with God, meets them from the other side of death?' At this period Lampe had not, it seems, entirely repudiated a doctrine of God as Three in One.

In *God as Spirit* we find very much the same sort of objections to the traditional christology. When people claim they encounter Jesus today, he says, they do not mean that they encounter a person of the first century AD. They mean they are meeting God in Jesus.[27] Again: 'To know Jesus Christ here and now is not to share the first disciples' experience of a personal presence'.[28] And later he writes: 'In order, then, to interpret God's saving work in Jesus we do not need the model of the descent of a pre-existent divine person into the world. Nor do we need the concept of a "post-existent' continuing personal presence of Jesus, himself alive to-day, in order to interpret our own continuing experience of God's saving and creative work.'[29]

So far then I might well claim Professor Lampe as an ally in presenting a non-traditional approach to the doctrine of the incarnation. He too sees the difficulties in the doctrine of hypostatic union, the impossibility of maintaining that we can have contact now with the human personality of Jesus, the dangers inherent in identifying Jesus with the eternal Son. Later on in the book, however, he develops his argument in a way which seems to lead him in a very different direction. He does not like the term Logos because it necessarily involves the notion of an hypostasis within the godhead, a suggestion which he now regards as leading to an unintelligible Trinitarian doctrine of God; and also because it tends to intellectualize Christian experience. He thinks it would have been better if the New Testament writers had used the term 'Spirit' for all manifestations of the godhead, whether before, during, or after the historical career of Jesus.[30] To this I think we must reply that the term Logos has its disadvantages, like every other word we have to use when talking about God, but that it did at least enable early Christians to speak about Jesus in terms of the closest relation to God without incurring the very natural accusation that they were preaching two gods. Some sort of doctrine of hypostasis within the godhead is necessary if this is to be done, and if Lampe rejects any notion of divine hypostasis we can only conclude that he is not prepared to associate Jesus sufficiently closely with the action of God – sufficiently closely, that is, to measure up to the standard of what the New Testament writers actually claim about Jesus.

Lampe suggests that the reason why Paul and John could not just identify the risen Christ with the Spirit was that they held a doctrine of the pre-existent Christ.[31] They therefore had to work out an ambiguous doctrine of the risen Christ experienced through the Spirit. And he adds that 'if Christ and the Holy Spirit are regarded as two co-existent beings it becomes impossible to assign to the Spirit a distinctive rôle in God's continuous and saving activity alongside the pre-existent and post-existent Christ'. Here we must distinguish. Paul certainly did think of a pre-existent Jesus Christ but it is not at all clear that John did, as I have tried to show in the last chapter, and this was precisely why he used a Logos doctrine. Also, the main and obvious reason why Paul and John have an account of the relation of the risen Christ to the

Spirit which is obscure is that they believed in the actual resurrection of Christ, which Lampe does not. To jettison any real belief in Christ's resurrection certainly simplifies one's christology, but it is a simplification which is bought at too high a price. I discuss the question of the relation of the Spirit to the risen Christ in the last chapter, and I hope to show that, though there certainly is an ambiguity about this doctrine in Paul, it has largely been cleared up in John, and that the subsequent development of the doctrine of the Spirit in the church completed the process of clarification.

Lampe produces further criticism of a Logos doctrine. The hypostatization of Logos leads ultimately, he says, to 'Christologies which make Jesus Christ seem painfully like a superman who invaded the planet Earth from outer space'.[32] This is certainly a valid criticism of the Alexandrian christology such as we meet, for example, in Athanasius' *De Incarnatione Verbi Dei*, but it is not true of all Logos doctrines. It is not true of Tillich's or Pittenger's, or of that put forward in *Grace and Truth*. Some of his criticism is valid only against those who try to maintain a traditional doctrine of a 'glorified humanity'. Thus, he claims later that there is an unanswerable question about the doctrine of the Trinity: 'What is the Spirit if it is "another" in relation to the Christ who reigns personally in heaven?'[33] I do not defend a doctrine of a Christ who reigns personally in heaven. At times Lampe exhibits a strange desire to be freed from the very particularity of Jesus. He writes: 'The more we come to discover about the real Jesus the more he is seen to be, as Schweitzer warned us long ago, a man of his own time; a stranger whom we cannot hope to understand.'[34] In so far as this is true at all, it is much more effective as an argument against the concept of a god-man, who might be expected to exhibit only universal human characteristics. It is much less effective against a doctrine of indwelling: there are features that distinguish all the saints. As Augustine said, *cor ad cor loquitur* across the ages. Equally strange is Lampe's attempt to by-pass to some degree the historicity of Christ. He argues that what really matters is what Christians have been inspired to think and say about Christ, not just what he actually did think and say: 'If a saying in the Gospels, such as for example one of the Beatitudes, touches the conscience and quickens the imagination of the readers, it does not greatly matter whether it was originally spoken by Jesus or by some unknown Christian prophet who shared "the mind of Christ".'[35]

On this argument we might well ask, how can you tell whether the early Christian prophet shared 'the mind of Christ', if you cannot distinguish between what he said and what Christ said?

Finally, some attention must be paid to Lampe's critique of the doctrine of the Trinity as such. He says, quite justly as it seems to me, that if you define 'person' in the Boethian sense of 'an individual substance of a rational nature', and apply that to the doctrine of the Trinity, you are bound to end in virtual tritheism.[36] He goes on to say that if you fall back on calling the three 'persons' relations, you must be able to say what is related. He claims that the classical answer to this consists in detailing abstract qualities, filiation, paternity, procession, etc., not Father, Son, and Holy Spirit, 'for there cannot be relations between the "three", each of which is identical not only with each of the others, but also with the whole triad'.[37] I wonder whether Lampe had given sufficient consideration to the account of the doctrine of the Trinity of Karl Barth and Karl Rahner, two theologians of sufficiently diverse traditions for there to be no danger of a narrow sectarian approach. Neither of these theologians would say that the Father was identical with the Son, nor the Son 'identical' with the Spirit. Identity precludes the possibility of distinction but there are distinctions within the godhead. Nor does the phrase 'mode of subsistence'[38] seem vulnerable to Lampe's criticism of 'relations' language. Later on he criticizes Karl Rahner for saying that the Trinity is based on 'our experience of Father, Son, and Spirit in salvation history', protesting that 'salvation history' means simply 'experience of Jesus Christ, identified with, and interpreted as, the pre-existent Son'.[39] But the concept of salvation history is not necessarily connected with a doctrine of a personally pre-existent Jesus Christ. It is true that I have argued in Chapter 2 that Paul and Hebrews accepted a doctrine of pre-existence because they wished (quite rightly) to integrate the Christ event into salvation history. But when John uses a Logos doctrine that does not necessarily require the concept of a personally pre-existent Jesus Christ, he is very far from jettisoning the idea of salvation history. On the contrary, salvation history, in the sense of the attempt to co-ordinate and integrate all God's revelatory actions in history with Israel culminating in Christ, is greatly illuminated and deepened by the doctrine of God as Three-in-One. We find, in fact, a triadic pattern in the divine action; God as source, God as redeemer, God active in those who respond to his redemptive action. We can have a Logos doctrine that does not involve the theory of an hypostatic union with its inevitable concomitant of some sort of docetism. We can have a Logos doctrine which explains the union of God and man in Jesus in terms compatible with our own experience. And we can have a doctrine of the Trinity which is mysterious indeed, as such a doctrine must necessarily be, but which does not involve either tritheism or the difficulties which Lampe sees in a relational account of the intra-Trinitarian situation.

Lampe has put his finger on a number of major difficulties in the traditional christology, but he has failed to find a sticking point between that christology and total Unitarianism. His Spirit-christology, in my opinion, fatally compromises the centrality and normativeness of Jesus Christ. What he obviously would have liked to have done cannot be achieved without a Logos doctrine, leading to a doctrine of God as Trinity.

I hold firmly therefore to a doctrine of the divine Word as revealed in Jesus Christ. In the most literal sense of the term, the Word became known in Jesus Christ. If it had not been for Jesus Christ, we would not have known that there were distinctions within the godhead, however much some traditions in Judaism may have seemed to be moving in this direction. The doctrine of the Logos in the early church was worked out because of the event of Jesus Christ. By the time that a doctrine of the Logos became current in the church's theology, Jesus Christ was securely established as central in the church's belief. Only because Christians wished to make sense of this belief was the doctrine of the divine Word elaborated. We could draw a parallel with the way in which in Old Testament times the character of God came gradually to be revealed. Early representation of God recorded in the Old Testament would hardly be recognizable as the God of Hosea, of the Second Isaiah, or the Book of Jonah. So with the doctrine of the Word of God and of the Trinity as a whole. Gradually as Christians realized the scope of the significance of Jesus Christ, they found themselves compelled to associate him with God to the point where they had to recognize distinctions within the godhead. The approach to the christology which I have outlined here allows for exactly the same necessity. This last consideration leads us on to the subject of the next chapter.

Six

The Anthropomorphic God

At the beginning of the last chapter I recorded that one of Brian Hebblethwaite's arguments in favour of the traditional christology concerned the question of whether God could suffer. He maintained that only the christology which he defended made adequate provision for the belief that God took upon himself the burden of our sorrows. In fact I agreed with Keith Ward that the traditional christology does not do this adequately, but this still leaves us with the question of the suffering of God. In *Grace and Truth*, Chapter 3, I tried to explain how my approach to the doctrine of the incarnation did actually allow us to say that in some sense God gave himself to us in the events of the life, death, and resurrection of Jesus Christ. But we have not yet considered whether we have made provision for the suffering of God in Jesus Christ. This is not just a question about God's act of suffering, but rather of whether we can say in any meaningful way that because we know God in Jesus Christ we know that he does enter into our sufferings. In other words, this is a question about the permanent meaning of Jesus Christ for Christians, not just about the actual events of the incarnation. It comes therefore more appropriately in this work than in *Grace and Truth*.

In this chapter I propose to maintain that Jesus Christ is the paramount pledge that God does share in our suffering. But in order to do this I must begin by examining carefully one passage in Hosea and two in Deutero-Isaiah. Such a reference back to the Old Testament should need no apology. Any adequate doctrine of the incarnation must be well rooted in the Old Testament, and I claimed in *Grace and Truth* that my approach to the doctrine was actually more firmly based on the Old Testament than was the traditional christology. If it can be shown that in the question of the suffering of God also we can appeal to Old Testament evidence, our alternative account of the incarnation will be established all the more securely.

The first passage is Hosea 11.1–9. For the purposes of this study I quote verses 1–4 and 8–9:

> When Israel was a child, I loved him,
>   and out of Egypt I called my son.
> The more I called them, the more they went from me;
>   they kept sacrificing to the Baals, and burning incense to idols.
> Yet it was I who taught Ephraim to walk,
>   I took them up in my arms;
>   but they did not know that I healed them.
> I led them with cords of compassion,
>   with the bands of love,
> and I became to them as one who eases the yoke on their jaws,
>   and I bent down to them and fed them.
>
> How can I give you up, O Ephraim!
>   How can I hand you over, O Israel!
> How can I make you like Admah!
>   How can I treat you like Zeboiim!
> My heart recoils within me,
>   my compassion grows warm and tender.
> I will not execute my fierce anger,
>   I will not again destroy Ephraim;
> for I am God and not man,
>   the Holy One in your midst,
>   and I will not come to destroy.

In verses 1–4 God describes how he called Israel in the infancy of the nation from Egypt: 'out of Egypt I called my son'. He protests that throughout Israel's history the tendency has been to ignore the call. He elaborates the description of Israel's up-bringing and probably uses also the figure of the farmer who treats his oxen with mercy. Verses 5–7 are a description of the punishment that Israel has brought on itself by its disobedience. Then in verse 8 a reaction occurs. God asks how he can bring himself to abandon Israel to the punishment it deserves. With bold anthropomorphism Hosea writes:

My heart recoils within me,
   my compassion grows warm and tender.

God declares he will not after all execute his immediate intention of destroying Israel, and the reason for this is given in a most remarkable way:

for I am God and not man,
   the Holy One in your midst.

The strongly anthropopathic account of God's changing his mind is explained by the very fact that God is not man.

A few critical details relating to this magnificent passage should be noted before we consult the experts about its theological content. All editors seem to be agreed that the correct translation of verse 2a is:

The more I called them,
   the more they went from me,

though this rendering means following the Greek rather than the Hebrew. In verse 4cd some editors reject the image of the farmer looking after the welfare of his oxen, and claim instead that we should see in it the image of a man holding a very small child up to his cheek as a mark of affection. Verse 4e then pictures the father as bending down to see the child take his food. This view is followed by Wolff and Mays.[1] Whichever way we understand this verse, it does not make any difference to the relevance of this passage as far as our purpose is concerned, but on the whole it seems better to retain the image of the farmer with his oxen. G. A. Smith thinks of 'a team of oxen mounting some steep road'.[2] Verse 7, we may virtually conclude, is hopelessly corrupt. Does it describe Israel's apostasy, or the effect of it, or Israel's attempts to free themselves from it (this last is W. Rudolph's suggestion[3])? We will ignore it in our consideration of the passage. The last line of verse 9 is also uncertain. The Hebrew 'into the city' does not make sense. It must express the same sentiment as 9ab, and most editors accept the RSV rendering:

and I will come to destroy.

We turn now to the detailed exegesis of Hosea 11.1–9. Of verse 1 Wolff well remarks: 'The first event in the life of young Israel is that Yahweh loves him.' It is, he thinks, the relationship of a father to an adopted son. He cites an instance, occurring a century later than Hosea, in which Bel is represented as saying to Esarhaddon of Assyria 'When you were small, I sustained you'. He believes that Hosea is struggling against Canaanite mythology: Israel is Yahweh's legitimate son, but the Israelites behave like bastards. Mays would render verse 1 'I came to love him'. He comments that Hosea portrays 'Israel as a young boy and God himself as a man who comes to love the lad and makes him his son'. Verse 3 describes a man teaching a small child to walk. So far, then, we have a picture of God choosing Israel, caring for him, and making plain his love for him. It is a process of education with Israel growing in knowledge of God.

We now consider verse 8. It begins dramatically with the Hebrew word '*eyik*, 'how?'. The Book of Lamentations begins with the same word in an emphatic form, and this has given its name to the book in Hebrew. Rudolph points out, however, that here in Hosea it means not a cry of lament but rather 'How is it possible . . . ?' Admah and Zeboiim in this verse are legendary cities of destruction like Sodom and Gomorrah. The last two lines of this verse literally translated would be:

> My heart has turned upon me,
>   my comfort grows warm together.

We must tread carefully when we are dealing with a very concrete language such as Hebrew, that does not possess a large number of synonyms. The word *lebb* ('heart') here means much more than 'heart' conveys in English, where it has a strong emotional overtone. In Hebrew it can mean 'mind, intention'. Wolff insists that the word which I have rendered with 'comfort', and which the RSV translates with 'compassion', should be understood as 'remorse'. 'His remorse (over his wrathful intention to judge) grows hot, i.e. it provokes and dominates him. . . . Again and again we see the God of Hosea in conflict with himself over Israel.'

Of verse 8 Harper says: 'Here begins the struggle in the prophet's mind between what seems to be the demand of justice and the claim of love.' It is interesting that he locates it in the prophet's mind. Yet he would not deny that the struggle in the prophet's mind reflects the struggle in God's mind. Weiser in similar vein remarks that Hosea's expression of the divine love in the face of Israel's disobedience is shaped and enhanced by his own experience.[4] 'The language', he continues, 'so anthropomorphically expressed, in which the peculiarly symbolic experience of the prophet is echoed, allows the greatness and the living, active power of God's love to appear, that love which, even in judgement, describes the ultimate ground of his dealings with Israel.' He goes on to say that the ultimate ground of God's dealings with Israel is not anger but 'unfathomable love' (*die unergründliche Liebe*). 'God's anger does not deaden his love, it is only another aspect of the one divine basic intention which God has never abandoned as far as his people is concerned.' Wolff claims that God's righteous will (which is how he renders *lebh*) is directed against himself, i.e. against his wrath. Rudolph actually uses the word 'anthropopathic': 'The prophet lives in such living personal relationship with his God that he does not shrink from such humanising expressions' (*Vermenschlichungen*). Mays points out that according to Deuteronomy 21.18–21 a disobedient son is to be put to death by stoning: 'Yahweh speaks of himself in the human genre to disclose in emotional terms that his election of Israel is stronger than their sin.'

Editors all make the same comment about verse 9, i.e. that God is not like man because he does not allow his wrath to divert him from his purpose of love. Weiser believes that this emphasis on the unchanging love of God obviates the danger that the boldly anthropomorphic language should produce a humanization of God. In fact, however, Hosea betrays no consciousness whatever of being embarrassed by the boldly anthropomorphic language which he uses. As Mays remarks à propos verse 7: 'Anthropomorphism is Hosea's stock-in-trade.' Wolff says that 'God proves himself to be God and the Holy One in Israel in that he, unlike men, is independent of his partner's actions. Remaining completely sovereign over his own actions, he is not compelled to react.' He adds that God's holiness, mentioned only here in Hosea, 'provides the foundation not for his judging will but for his saving will to which he has committed himself from the very beginning of Israel's saving history'. His final comments are very significant: 'What is to determine Israel's future, Israel's own rejection of Yahweh or Yahweh's love? . . . Yahweh cannot set aside his love just as he cannot set aside his divinity . . . the destructive "overturning" and "burning" of judgment against Admah and Zeboiim now takes place in God's heart instead of in Israel' (we have noticed that in verse 8 God's heart literally 'turns over' and his compassion 'grows hot'). Rudolph remarks that it is astonishing that 'Hosea sees in God's holiness the loving aspect of his being. He is in their midst just because he is the loving God'. He calls this 'Evangelium im Alten Testament'. In much the same way Mays writes: 'God's wrath is his active refusal to let Israel go her own way oblivious of his claim upon her, and therefore is an expression of the election of Israel. . . . The apparent inconsistency is a warning that Hosea's many anthropomorphisms are meant as inter-pretative analogies, not as essential definitions. . . . Yahweh's refusal to destroy Israel is no concession to their sin, no curtailment of discipline.'

We must return to Hosea later, when we have tried to put these and other Old Testament passages in their true context as far as concerns the doctrine of the incarnation. Here we may content ourselves with noting three points. First, God's experience is reflected in the prophet's experience. We could not have known God's feelings towards Israel if the prophet had not first experienced an analogous relationship in his own life. This is not to adopt the Freudian conclusion that Hosea is merely projecting his own feelings on to a God of his own invention. But the actual process by which God's will for Israel, and his revelation of his character to Israel, became known necessarily involved a domestic tragedy in Hosea's life. In a limited sense Hosea had to live out in his own life God's relationship to Israel.

Second, there is a hint of conflict within God himself. Indeed there is more than a hint, for verse 8 boldly declares that God's love has overcome his wrath. We are in very deep waters here, for Hosea is attributing to God what looks on the surface like inconstancy. The editors, as we have seen, make strenuous, and largely successful, efforts to explain this charge away. God is not inconstant, because his wrath is an expression of his love. But, whatever these expressions really mean, they are put in a form which makes it difficult to avoid the conclusion that Hosea at least had no difficulty in thinking of God as being at odds with himself. Wolff, as we have seen, believes that according to Hosea God is 'in conflict with himself'. We may at least say this much: the cost of Israel's disobedience is borne by God himself. We are reminded of R. C. Moberly's analogy for the doctrine of the atonement, in which he gives the example of the parents of a delinquent youngster who are, in fact, far more grieved about the damage which the youngster has inflicted than he is himself.[5] But perhaps we have entered the area of the doctrine of the atonement, with which we are not directly concerned.

Thirdly, we must be impressed with the fact that Hosea gives as the reason why God's love overcomes his wrath that he is God and not man. In other words, a striking anthropomorphism is justified by the fact that God is not like man! Surely this must convince us that for Hosea at least – and this probably applies to all the great prophets of of the Old Testament – anthropomorphism was not regarded as a weakness, or a danger, or an artificial way of speaking about God, but as a necessity if God is to be spoken about with truth and effectiveness. We may indeed protest that Hosea and the other prophets in using these anthropomorphic expressions are employing poetic language. But this does not explain anything. Poetic language can still convey truth. Poetry is not simply a fancy way of saying something that could just as well be said in plain prose. It is an idiom which is peculiarly appropriate for conveying certain forms of truth, and truth about God seems to be one of these forms. If anthropomorphic expressions are necessarily used by the greatest writers of the Old Testament in speaking about God's character, it seems very appropriate that the supreme expression of God's character should meet us in the form of a human life. Anthropomorphism is not a concession to the weakness of the human intellect, or a fancy way of expressing principles about God that could be set out in plain philosophical terms. It is the chosen mode for God's revelation of himself. He has chosen to express himself through the form of a man. He is the anthropomorphic God.

We must now look at two passages in Deutero-Isaiah, in the first of which we have further bold anthropomorphisms used, and in the second of which we seem to approach again to the thought of God suffering with his people. The first is Isaiah 42.13–14:

> The Lord goes forth like a mighty man,
>   like a man of war he stirs up his fury;
> he cries out, he shouts aloud,
>   he shows himself mighty against his foes.

For a long time I have held my peace,
  I have kept myself still and restrained myself;
now I will cry out like a woman in travail,
  I will gasp and pant.

K. Elliger is uncertain whether the word rendered 'fury' here (*qin'ah*) means God's own desire for battle or the desire of those who are to follow him.[6] The word indicates passion, positive or negative. The cry which God utters can mean the battle-cry or the paean of victory. Elliger thinks the prophet has in mind Cyrus' victorious army. Knight says God's *qin'ah* is his burning purpose of love[7]. God the warrior is marching on, so is Israel. And so, we may conjecture, is the prophet, in spirit at least. His further comment is very significant for the purpose of our study: 'By such language (Deutero-Isaiah) shocks his readers into recognising that God is not beyond the pain which his people is even then suffering but must be One with them as they meet the judgement which God himself has caused.'[8] It is doubtful whether those who first heard Deutero-Isaiah speaking in these terms would have been shocked at the anthropomorphism as such. Knight seems to be attributing to those for whom Deutero-Isaiah prophesied a squeamishness about anthropomorphisms that is only appropriate for those who have inherited Greek cultural traditions. Bonnard is more accurate: 'These anthropomorphisms perhaps shock us. In fact they are precious first because they teach us that God is neither distant nor uninterested, nor indifferent to the misery of the world; and next because they prepare us the better to understand the incarnation of the Son of God, who must die in order to bring the Church to birth.'[9] He has seen the connection with the incarnation, but it is doubtful whether he has pressed the analogy sufficiently far. God's anthropomorphism is mirrored in the lives of the men and women whom he calls: here it is Cyrus who is primarily in mind but also perhaps Israel, who must wake up from the sleep of despair and prepare to play her part in the theatre of action which God has devised for her. We may reasonably conclude that the prophet himself has experienced something of what it means to wake out of sleep and join in vigorous action. Certainly we can say of his stirring call to Israel to respond to God's initiative: 'he cries out, he shouts aloud'. In other words, God's intentions and thoughts are expressed through the actions and words of men and women whom he calls. If the time was to come when he should express himself supremely, we would by the analogy of passages such as these expect it to be done by means of a human life completely and supremely dedicated to him.

There seem to be two elements to be distinguished in verse 14: on the one hand there is a contrast between God's long silence and apparent inactivity as far as Israel's sufferings are concerned. This is illustrated by the sudden onset of a woman's labour: a long period of quiet gestation followed by a sudden crisis marked by sharp cries and groans. Westermann seems to think that this is the only point of the simile here.[10] On the other hand there is the thought of something new coming to birth. This aspect is emphasized by Elliger. Whybray, rightly no doubt, retains both elements: 'The simile of the woman in travail, which is reinforced in the Hebrew by a breathless and convulsive style which seems ugly to modern western taste, is intended to convey not only a sudden burst of noise and commotion but also the idea that something new is about to be born – these are the "birthpangs of God" (Muilenburg).'[11]

The simile of the woman labouring to bring forth a child is used elsewhere in Jewish-Christian literature. It occurs in the *Hymns of Thanksgiving* of the Qumran sectaries about the coming into existence of the messianic community (IQH 3.7–12); and in Revelation 12.1–6 of the birth of the Messiah. Here it is used with impressive boldness for God as he carries out his plans for Israel. This is just one more proof of the fact that the great prophets never hesitated to use strongly anthropomorphic language in order to express God's intentions. They seem to have no notion of either of the impassibility of God, or of his dignity in the Aristotelian sense. The Targum, written in a later and less free-spoken era, cannot tolerate the boldness of the metaphor, and paraphrases so that it is Israel who is compared to a woman in labour.

The second passage in Deutero-Isaiah is 43.22–24:

> Yet you did not call upon me, O Jacob;
> but you have been weary of me, O Israel!
> You have not brought me your sheep for burnt offerings,
>   or honoured me with your sacrifices.
> I have not burdened you with offerings,
>   or wearied you with frankincense.

You have not bought me sweet cane with money,
    or satisfied me with the fat of your sacrifices.
But you have burdened me with your sins,
    you have wearied me with your iniquities.

All the experts seem to agree that the prophet is minimizing the value of
the sacrificial cultus which Israel had maintained before the exile. All
the prophets insisted, says Elliger, that the cult treated sin much too
lightly. Knight claims that the meaning is this: the exile put an end to
the sacrificial cultus. This was an opportunity for Israel to learn that
she can know God without it. Instead of that she concluded that the
covenant was abrogated and has given herself over to despair. Bonnard
sees an implicit protest on the part of Israel: 'We have lavished offerings
upon you, and look what you have done to us!' Yahweh replies that
he never asked them to go to all this needless trouble. Westermann
considers that according to Deutero-Isaiah the cult during the monar-
chical period was a mistaken way of approaching God.

In verse 24c 'You have burdened me with your sins' is literally 'You
have made me to serve', which the Vulgate renders with 'servire me
fecisti in peccatis tuis'. The verb used in the word translated 'you have
wearied me with your iniquities' in verse 24d (*yaga'* used in Hiph'il)
may indicate forced labour. The Targum renders:

    but thou hast multiplied thy transgressions before me,
    and thou hast pressed hard upon me [lit. before me] with thine
       iniquities[12]

Traditional Jewish exegesis could hardly accept the idea of God being
turned into a servant because of Israel's sins, but they could allow a
measure of constraint. In *Pesikta Rabbati* we read: 'In another comment
the words are rendered *But thou hast burdened me with thy sins* (Isaiah
43.24). By these words the Holy One, blessed be he, meant: because of
your sins you made me assume the burden of exile in Babylon, as is
said, "Because of you I had Myself to go to Babylon" ' (sic).[13] The
reference is to Isaiah 43.24. Here is the concept of God suffering with
(though not exactly for) Israel.

Knight quite explicitly finds here the idea of God suffering for
Israel: 'It was he alone who was now bearing the sacrificial cost of the

union. . . . It is God himself then who is thus in an ultimate sense *the Servant* that Israel had been called and chosen to be. . . . But the work of (Deutero-Isaiah) reveals to us the sufferings of a God who wills to suffer.' If this is not overinterpreting this passage, it looks as though we have in Second Isaiah Israel as the servant, the Servant as the servant (whoever he was, perhaps the prophet himself), and even (here) God as the servant. Once again we see the pattern that God's character is revealed in the life of his servants. Bonnard goes even further: ' "The servant is not greater than his master", Jesus will say, Jesus, who will bear the sins of the world in order to take them away, and who will invite his friends to do as he does, in order to conform themselves to the Servant-God or Slave-God of his rebellious children.'[14]

At least we may say of this last passage that the notion of God suffering because of his people's sins is here in Deutero-Isaiah; and we may add that it is known and conveyed to us only because the prophet himself first shared in that suffering.

This anthropomorphism found in the writings of the great prophets must be placed in its context in the development of the doctrine of the incarnation. To begin with, it must be emphasized again that such anthropomorphism is not the same as the primitive anthropomorphism of earlier parts of the Old Testament, such as God being represented as shutting the door of the ark in Genesis 7.16; or his smelling the pleasing odour of Noah's sacrifice in Gen. 8.21; or God being dissuaded from his intention to destroy Israel by an appeal to his vanity as in Exodus 32.7–14; or God being represented as instigating Saul to sin, as in I Sam. 26.19. This anthropomorphic language of the great prophets is poetic, not primitive. They are saying something about God that perhaps could not be said by any other means. Poetry uses the language of simile, metaphor, analogy, not just as a decoration but as a serious means of expression. It is true that the prophets do this quite unselfconsciously. We, with our sophisticated background of Greek rationalism and scientific literalism, find it difficult to put ourselves mentally back into the period of the great prophets. But if we are to understand what they are saying we must accept that their anthropomorphisms were neither primitive survivals nor deliberate artifice. They are the technique of expression which came naturally to them, and unless we can accept it without intellectual condescension we cannot hope fully to receive their message.

But when Israel passed under Greek imperial government, they encountered for the first time the challenge of rational philosophical thought. By the time the Ptolemaic empire was established the Greeks had already produced Plato and Aristotle. Any system of religion would be bound to be subjected to the scrutiny of the philosophers. Any young educated Israelite who had the opportunity of absorbing the new, exciting culture must be driven to ask himself painful questions about his own religious tradition. Greek philosophy had not as yet worked out anything like a theology, but it had evolved certain principles which must have put questions marks against the Hebrew concept of God. Both the Platonic and the Aristotelian tradition held that God belonged to the sphere of the intellect and both concluded (for rather different reasons) that God could not be deeply concerned with mundane matters or with human history. The Platonic tradition said that such things as history and sensible objects were unreal and the divine (they preferred to call God *to theion*) was ultimate reality. The Aristotelian tradition said that the Unmoved Mover was absorbed in pure thought and was therefore totally unaware of the world. In the course of the third century BC Stoicism came into prominence as an alternative to the two major philosophical traditions. Though its founder, Zeno of Citium, may have been a Semite rather than a Greek, there was nothing Hebrew about his concept of God. His God was a sort of world-stuff and was just as incompatible with Hebrew ideas as anything that Plato or Aristotle produced. None of these three traditions could have been able to make any sense of the sort of anthropomorphic language used by Hosea and Deutero-Isaiah. They would have dismissed the passages we have been considering as the figments of poets, not to be taken seriously by philosophers.

No doubt many educated Jews under Greek rule simply gave up their ancestral religion. This was the process known as Hellenizing. It happened to every other culture affected by Greek civilization, including the Roman. The astonishing thing is that it did not simply abolish Hebrew religion. That religion survived and even managed to make some attempts to counter-attack. But in order to do so it had to borrow the enemy's own weapons. Only those who had studied Greek philosophy could hope to answer the challenge of Greek philosophy from the side of Hebrew belief in God. In the process of answering the challenge the champions of Hebrew belief were themselves altered.

The challenge, we may note, was not to Hebraize the Greek world, a task which almost no Jew would envisage, far less attempt, but to preserve within Israel a belief in Israel's God which would not be dismissed by Greek-educated Israelites as crude and unscientific. It was a battle for the soul of Israel, not for the soul of the world.

The first signs of the attempt to meet the challenge appear in Proverbs 8 and in Qoheleth. Both these writings are put by most scholars in the Greek period. The first is still very much in the vein of poetry: wisdom's account of her part in the creation of the world is written in Hebrew poetic form. But it does perhaps reflect a desire to allow room for the divine reason in the universe. Qoheleth is more obscure and has almost no guidance to give. But he seems to be trying to use Hebrew words in a philosophical way. Perhaps all that we can say about the author of Ecclesiastes is that he is aware of the problem, and does not solve it by Hellenizing. Jesus ben Sira is very much in the tradition of Proverbs 8. Nobody could call Ecclesiasticus 24 a philosophical document, but at least it continues the wisdom tradition and attempts to relate Israel to God's purpose in terms which connect it with his purpose in creation. Perhaps we have here the germ of a philosophy of religion.

The Book of Wisdom is very interesting from our point of view, because the author tries to maintain a belief in the God of Hosea and Deutero-Isaiah without repudiating the insights of Greek philosophy.[15] It is true that he does not seem to have been very deeply read in Greek philosophy, but he at least knew the technical terms of Stoic thought (Wisdom 7.22); he was aware of the Platonic conviction that the body is an obstacle to the right functioning of the soul (9.15); he could use *pneuma*, *logos*, and *sophia* as terms which mediate between God and the world. We can hardly describe him as a successful reconciler of Hebrew and Greek thought, but at least he succeeded in believing both in the God of the great prophets and in *to theion* as expounded by what corresponded to the sixth-form teachers of philosophy in Alexandria in the first century before Christ.

Less than a hundred years later, in all probability, there appeared one much more competent to expound the God of Israel in terms of Greek philosophy. Philo of Alexandria really knew his contemporary philosophy. If the author of the Book of Wisdom writes at university entrance standard, Philo must be regarded as a doctor of philosophy. He could handle Plato, Aristotle, and Zeno, at least in the form known to his contemporaries. He knew his Middle Platonism. He could write like a Greek philosopher. At the same time, he earnestly desired to be a devout Jew, faithful to the Torah. He was convinced that the Jewish religious tradition contained everything of value that any Greek thinker had ever conceived of, if only it could be extracted from the writings of Moses. His solution to the problem of how to reconcile Greek ideas about *to theion* with the Hebrew concept of God on the whole resolved itself into the claim that there was a transcendent, unknowable, Greek type of God existing in the sphere of *theoria*, but that the Hebrew characteristics of God were represented by intermediate entities, primarily the Logos, but also by what he called the 'powers' (*dunameis*), the divine mind (*nous*), and the divine wisdom (*sophia*). This solution to the problem was of great significance to Christianity (which was actually being born during the closing years of Philo's lifetime), for two reasons. First, it provided Christian theologians with a good deal of their vocabulary. I have already claimed that the author of Colossians drew on Philo's tradition.[16] And secondly Philo provided an alternative solution to that which orthodox Christian theology chose. Philo was the grandfather of Arianism, and constituted a standing temptation to Christian theologians for the next five hundred years.

By the end of the first century AD Christianity was face to face with essentially the same problem as that which Philo tackled, how to reconcile the active, living, suffering God of the great prophets with what Greek philosophy said the divine principle must be like. But the problem was accentuated for Christian theologians by something which was in fact a swing back towards the higher anthropomorphism of the prophets. This was the career of Jesus Christ. Christians saw in Jesus Christ the supreme manifestation of God's activity and character. Jesus had lived a fully human life, had exhibited human emotions, had suffered, and died. Hence Christianity was bound to represent a revindication of that 'poetic' element in Israel's understanding of God which we have traced in Hosea and Deutero-Isaiah. God, it seems, could feel emotion, could suffer, could perhaps even die. Indeed the kernel of the Christian message was that God had done all these things in Jesus Christ.

How were intelligent educated Christians to cope with this? The career of Jesus Christ might well have seemed to make the problem more difficult the more Christians affirmed that Jesus Christ really was

God, the more difficult they found it to say that God had experienced emotion, suffered, died. In fact Christian thinkers followed one of two courses, both of which could claim some support within the New Testament:

(a) They chose Philo's solution: the suffering and dying was done not by *to theion* but an inferior intermediary who was sufficiently like God to make it plausible to say that God had suffered these experiences. This was the Arian solution. It was rejected by the church in the course of the fourth century AD. It could appeal perhaps to the implied christology of Hebrews, even possibly to Paul's christology, though this is much more obscure. It seems likely that the christological formula in I Timothy 2.5 has Arian implications, though they were certainly not recognized by the author of the Pastorals.[17]

(b) Alternatively they chose a two-natures theory. According to this account, God had indeed been personally present in Jesus, but the emotion, suffering, and dying were not experienced by the divine nature, but by the human. This was the Chalcedonian solution. It could appeal with a good deal of plausibility to the Fourth Gospel, though it is by no means demonstratively certain that this was the direction in which John's christology was moving. This solution enabled theologians, with far more conviction than in the Arian tradition, to maintain that God had really shared our human condition, and even that the poetic language about God used by the prophets made sense even for those trained in Greek rational philosophy. Whether you followed the Antiochene or the Alexandrian tradition, you could still claim that in some sense God had suffered and died. It was, admittedly, more difficult for the Antiochenes. Eustathius, an extreme Nestorian, may well have let the cat out of the bag when he said of John 20.17 that this was not uttered by the Logos but by the Man.[18] Indeed on a strict Antiochene interpretation you could only say 'God suffered and died' by a sort of linguistic convention. In practice the human nature was there in order to act as a shield to protect the divine nature from all such human experiences.

Perhaps the Alexandrian tradition fared better in this respect. But when you examine them closely the Alexandrian theologians are just as chary of attributing human emotions and experiences to God as are the Antiochenes. They tended to deny the actuality of the human experience of Jesus and thereby to impugn the reality of the human nature.

But at the last analysis they too could only bring themselves to say 'God suffered and died' by a *façon de parler*. Christian theologians of the first five hundred years of the church's history had to use the language of Greek philosophy. If they wished to produce an intelligible doctrine of God they had no other option. But at the end of the day they did not really succeed in reconciling the fine, free, poetic anthropomorphism of the great prophets with their own basically Greek presuppositions. The most that they succeeded in doing was to ensure that this anthropomorphic element in God should not completely drop out of sight.

The Jewish theological tradition continued on its way independently of Philo, who was, in effect, taken over by the Christians. The Rabbis lived for the most part in the Graeco-Roman world and could not help being affected by the culture of that world, but they did not allow it to affect their theology. In fact they did not attempt to meet the challenge of Greek rational philosophy of religion. As one reads the Talmud and the pesiktas, one feels oneself nearer to the world of Hosea and Deutero-Isaiah than to that of Plato and Aristotle. The Rabbis do not at all mind attributing emotion to the Holy One, blessed be He. They draw the line at certain anthropomorphisms in the scriptures, such as the suggestion that God could be found in one place, for example, but they make no attempt to work out a rationally intelligible doctrine of God. Moltmann refers to the work of Abraham Heschel, who claims that in the prophets the divine suffering is not identical with his being, but is the form of his relationship to others. God, he says, is interested in the world to the point of suffering. But Maimonides and Spinoza, influenced by the Greek tradition in theology, held that strictly speaking God neither loves nor hates. Greek philosophy had to overtake Judaism eventually.[19]

How does this discussion help us in our problem today? It reinforces the contention that the only way God can be meaningfully said to feel human emotion and to suffer is in the persons of his servants. We do know in our experience how God can express himself through the saints. That is our best guide as to how he expressed himself supremely through Jesus Christ. We can use such great prophets as Hosea and Deutero-Isaiah as our markers. When Hosea said that God's love overcame his anger, Hosea himself experienced this. Indeed he goes out of his way to tell us how his domestic experience mirrors the experience of God with Israel. When Deutero-Isaiah says that God is rousing himself, is labouring like a woman with child, this tension was first exhibited in the experience of the prophet himself. Remarkably enough, it seems as if this is just the opposite to what Philo and even some traditions in the New Testament believed about the way in which prophecy worked. Philo firmly maintains that the prophets were mere mouthpieces of God, quite unaware of what they were saying and in no way masters of the contents of their message. The same view seems to be implied in II Peter 1.20–21; 2.16.[20] Exactly the opposite appears to be the truth: the prophet could only utter the word of God because he had experienced it first himself.

This is not to suggest that the meaning of Hosea 11 is exhausted in the statement that Hosea found in his domestic life that his love overcame his anger. Rather, Hosea's experience accurately reflects something analogous in God. So with Jesus: his experience of love, grief, rejection, suffering, even death, accurately reflects something real in God. But we do not need to say that therefore Jesus was God in an ontological sense, because if we do so we find that either we end by saying that God did not really have these experiences, or the statement becomes meaningless.

I have already quoted Mays as saying that 'Hosea's many anthropomorphisms are meant as interpretative analogies, not as essential definitions'.[21] This is a pregnant phrase. Can we apply it to the doctrine of the incarnation? The entire career of Jesus is an 'interpretative analogy' for the intention, and hence the character, of God. It is not an 'essential definition' in the sense that we cannot say Jesus Christ *is* God. But he is the supreme interpretative analogy, in the sense that in him God has expressed, revealed, communicated himself to us as clearly, as closely as his nature permits. There is no way by which he could have revealed himself more clearly. Hosea represents God as in some sense feeling within himself the pain of Israel's disobedience. His own experience of distress and grief at his wife's behaviour is the means by which God's pain was mediated to him and therefore to us. May we not regard the passion and death of Jesus Christ in the same way? Just as Hosea's domestic experience was an extrapolation of God's grief at Israel's disobedience, so the cross may be regarded as the extrapolation of God's reaction to man's sin. In the cross we are assured of God's suffering because of man's sin, and are moreover invited to share in that suffering ourselves. The incarnation is a necessary recall to the anthropomorphic method of understanding God practised by the great prophets. The cross is the permanent symbol and pledge to mankind that God suffers with them and for them.

It is very interesting to turn at this point to the work of a distinguished modern Jewish scholar, already referred to above, who has dealt at length with very much the topic of this chapter. A. J. Heschel, in his book *The Prophets*[22], has devoted an entire chapter to what he calls the 'pathos' of God. By this he means the way in which the prophets consistently represent God as experiencing human emotions. He claims that this pathos of God is not an abstract attribute: 'Pathos is not an ultimate but a situation'.[23] It really means 'God as involved in history'.[24] He writes: 'Just because it is not a final reality, but a dynamic modality, does pathos make possible a living encounter between God and his people.' Pathos is concerned with 'the unique, the specific, and the particular'.[25] Heschel claims that pathos is much more appropriate to a covenant relationship than to a merely legal tie. It suggests 'a dynamic multiplicity of forms of relationship'.[26] He repeats that pathos is not 'an essential attribute of God ... but an expression of God's will ... it is a functional rather than a substantial reality'.[27] His last word is: 'The prophets never identify God's pathos with his essence, because for them the pathos is not something absolute, but a form of relation ... the real basis between God and man'.[28]

Though no doubt Rabbi Heschel would have repudiated the idea, this theory of the pathos of God brings him in certain respects quite close to a doctrine of incarnation. The anthropomorphism of the prophets is their way of indicating God's involvement in history. But the Christian claim is that God's supreme involvement in history took a supremely anthropomorphic form, but not one that is so completely *sui generis* as to have no presentiments in Israel's history. Indeed the remarkable phrase which Heschel uses at one point 'a dynamic modality' actually recalls that Modalism which was one of the unsuccessful attempts in the early church to express a satisfactory doctrine of the Trinity. Or else it reminds us of the Eastern Orthodox doctrine, mentioned above, which holds that we can only perceive God's activity in the world by means of his 'energies' which are not part of his essence. According to Heschel the strongly anthropomorphic element in the prophets' description of God's activity is the basis for his relationship to man. Hence, if we wish to move towards the centre of God as related to men, we must move in what we might call an anthropo-morphic direction.

It is also surely significant for our study that Heschel rejects any suggestion that the pathos of God is of his essence. To this corresponds our claim that the incarnation should not be expressed in substantialist terms, but in terms of a relation of indwelling and grace between the Word and Jesus.

We conclude therefore that the higher anthropomorphism of the great prophets, far from representing a crude stage of apprehension of God which we have outgrown, enshrines something of vital importance about God, and finds its supreme expression in the life of Jesus under-stood as the reflection and revelation of God's character. We can use Hosea's description of God's reaction to Israel's situation in the eighth century before Christ as an analogy for the doctrine of the incarnation. But we do not present a picture of a God-man who eventually gives us a satisfactory account neither of God nor of man. Admittedly today we are not committed to the concept of a wholly transcendent, impassible, impersonal divine principle (*to theion*) in the way that the Fathers were. But this does not mean that we can happily revert to the concept of a God who literally and in person grows angry, grieves, suffers and dies. We still need to believe in a God who is behind the universe, a God whom modern scientists (physicists at least) seem to require more than ever if they are to make sense of their findings. Indeed recent develop-ments in the philosophy of science suggest that science may find that it urgently needs the concept of a God of love in order to resist the efforts of those who wish to turn it into a tool for the holders of power. We also need, in the sphere of philosophy, a God who gives meaning to the world and life, in fact a Logos. The polarity between the personal, active, living God of the Hebrew higher anthropomorphism and the unchanging divine principle behind the universe is still there. But I believe it can be greatly eased by the approach to the doctrine of the incarnation which I have outlined and especially by the realization that a certain anthropomorphism in our account of God is both required by the witness of the scriptures and is in accordance with the deepest significance of the doctrine of the incarnation.

At one point in II Corinthians 3 Paul contrasts Moses' veiling of his face, so that the Israelites should not see the glory of the Lord revealed in the tabernacle, with the freedom (*parrhesia*) which he and his fellow-workers enjoy. That word *parrhesia* really means free speech, boldness in utterance. The doctrine of the incarnation should be in some sense a healthy return to that boldness of speech which the prophets used. Because God has in Jesus Christ shown himself to be the anthropomorphic God, we are no longer restricted to the concept of a God who is wholly transcendent, impassible, incapable of change. God known in the form of Jesus Christ means that we need not be afraid of conceiving him as suffering, as active, as accommodating himself to our condition. Jesus Christ, we may be sure, corresponds to and reflects something real in God. The divine Word chose him to be the mirror of his own character. Because he is the reflection of God, we can boldly speak of God experiencing such emotions as love, of God suffering, of God giving himself for us.

We must thus regard the language which the New Testament writers use about Jesus Christ as forming a sort of climax or culmination of what was already known about God in Israel. The incarnation was not the irruption of something entirely new. It was more the full revelation of what was always there, about which the greatest spirits in Israel already knew something. We might test this statement by taking one or two crucial statements about Jesus Christ made in the New Testament and asking ourselves whether Israel could ever have said anything like this about Adonai.

(a) 'Behold the Lamb of God, who takes away the sin of the world!' (John 1.29). There is some reason to think that what the author of the Fourth Gospel meant by *ho airōn* ('who takes away') was more like 'who bears the sin of the world'.[29] If so, we can trace a connection with Isaiah 43.24, which we have examined above. God has been compelled (by his love, of course, not by any external necessity) to bear Israel's sins. The great difference between John 1.29 and Isaiah 43.24 does not lie in the thought of God bearing sin, but in the fact that Jesus bears the sin of the world, not just of Israel. This is indeed distinctive and is an important part of the uniqueness of the incarnation. But I think we can claim that there is no absolute difference here.

(b) 'He (God) who did not spare his only Son but gave him up for us all will he not also give us all things with him' (Rom. 8.32). This sounds very Christian and far from Jewish Monotheism. But we must bear in mind that 'Son' here is a metaphor. God does not literally have a son. His 'Son' is himself in his aspect as concerned with his creation and supremely with his creature man. So when we say God gave his only Son we mean that God gave himself, or we do not mean anything at all, if we are to continue to be monotheists. He did not spare himself in the face of our sinful condition. This is not the same thing as what Hosea says, but it is within measurable distance of it. Hosea says that in the face of Israel's persistent disobedience God does not cast Israel off. On the contrary, he bears the pain of Israel's wrongdoing himself. He gives himself to the task of winning her back, by means of painful discipline no doubt. This involves pain and suffering on God's part, an experience which is mediated to us by the pain and suffering of the prophet who delivers this message. In Jesus Christ God the Word gave himself to us in the sense that he declared God's willingness to suffer in order to win us back; he revealed his character of self-giving love to us supremely in the passion and death of Jesus Christ. 'The Holy One in your midst' (as Hosea puts it in 11.9) shows himself holy by the very fact that he is perfectly expressed in a human life. God manifesting his costly love for Israel through Hosea's experience and message can be seen to be the foreshadowing of God manifesting in an even more costly way his love for the whole world through the life, death and resurrection of Jesus Christ.

(c) 'But (Christ) emptied himself, taking the form of a servant, being born in the likeness of men' (Phil. 2.7). This is of course peculiarly appropriate to the incarnation and nothing else. But perhaps the elements can be found in the old dispensation. We have already seen how Isaiah 43.24 moved Bonnard to write of the Servant-God. God has already in the prophetic passages we have looked at been described in terms of human action. This is not just the obvious platitude that if we are to speak of God at all we must use human language. It is more than that: the prophets have deliberately described God's actions and purposes as if they were the actions and purposes of a man. Hence when he actually expresses himself to us in the life of one particular man he is not doing anything contrary to his known character. Perhaps even the fact that the prophet in Isaiah 42.14 chooses the simile of a woman in travail with child in order to convey to us that God is about to do some great new act may help us to see the true significance of the birth of this child Jesus, whose life, death, and resurrection are to constitute the greatest of all God's acts. As for 'he emptied himself', God does give himself to Israel in these prophetic passages. He suffers the pain of Israel's disobedience himself; he allows himself to be made to serve by their sins. The very fact that he has chosen Israel and will not let her go despite all her apostasies puts some sort of a voluntary restraint on God. As Karl Barth so finely puts it, God compromises himself for the sake of mankind. He pledged himself to Israel. He has pledged himself to us in Christ. Though we cannot accept the Kenotic notion of God the Son voluntarily foregoing some of his divine attributes in order to become incarnate, we can see in the fact that God chose supremely to reveal his character in the suffering and death of Jesus something of the divine self-giving. God gives himself in the obedience and suffering of his servants. He gave himself supremely in the one great Servant, Jesus Christ.

I end this chapter by dealing with two questions which arise in connection with our theme. The first is this: have we the right to universalize the sympathy of God by means of the particularity of Jesus? Hosea's experience was a pledge of God's unfailing love for Israel. How can Jesus be a pledge that God suffers with all men? In effect we must reply that Jesus was rejected by the leaders of Israel because of his message and mission, which led beyond Israel. He conceived his mission, it is true, as concerned with Israel only. It seems likely that he deliberately offered his life as a sacrifice on behalf of Israel. But the implications of his message and mission took his followers inevitably beyond the borders of Israel. This was because in the last analysis Jesus' message removed the Torah from the centre of Israel's religion. The coming kingdom, and not the Torah, was the important element in the relation between God and man, and if the two clashed, the demands of the Torah must give way to the demands of the kingdom. Jesus was convicted and put to death primarily because he seemed to be a threat to the religion of the Torah, and so in the deepest sense he was. It was because of his message, mission, death and resurrection that the knowledge of the God of Israel could be transmitted to the whole world. When Jesus was born it must have seemed that the God of Israel had been securely immured within the fence of the Torah. No one who was not willing to accept the whole Torah, ritual laws and all, could come to know the God of Israel. Through the death and resurrection of Jesus this knowledge became available to all. We may universalize the significance of Jesus' suffering and death because he was the means by which the knowledge of the true God became universalized.

The second question concerns the relevance of the concept of the anthropomorphic God to the theme of this book. We can claim if we like that the life, passion, and death of Jesus represent to us God's will to suffer with men. But is this not all in the past? Does it not all belong to the theme of *Grace and Truth* (the doctrine of the incarnation) rather than to the theme of this book, the relation of the ascended Christ to God and to believers? But here surely we are concerned with the meaning of our title: Jesus *is*, not was, the image of the invisible God. He is permanent symbol, pledge, and form of the God who wills to suffer for us and with us. This is essentially the same question as that discussed at the end of the last chapter, but expressed now in terms of the suffering of God. Jesus Christ is not just a good man who saw farther into the mind of God than others did. He is the chosen means of the self-communication of God the Word, and hence his cross (climax of his life and passion) is the form under which we apprehend the suffering of God. The cross is a symbol. There is no need to deny this. But it is an effective symbol. And here we may legitimately call in Paul's doctrine of the church as the body of Christ, and his concept of Christians as those who are called to reproduce in their own lives the life of Christ. The suffering of God in Christ is constantly represented, and to some degree can be experienced, in the suffering of the church, which is called to be his body. The divine Word has chosen this form, Christ crucified, in which to express his sharing in our suffering.

Seven

The Heavenly Intercession

There is one function traditionally ascribed to the ascended Christ which we have not yet considered. This is his heavenly intercession. This topic is not an easy one to discuss with any great clarity, because his function as intercessor is closely connected, if not identical, with the work of the Holy Spirit; and also because the work of intercession tends to be associated with the work of propitiation, and we find our-selves in the middle of an exposition of the doctrine of the atonement.

I propose to begin by examining the doctrine of the heavenly inter-cession in Paul, Hebrews, and the Fourth Gospel. This will mean con-sidering the doctrine of the Spirit in these three New Testament writings at the same time. The two topics cannot be separated. I hope to show that there is considerable confusion in the minds of Paul and the author of Hebrews as far as distinguishing the work of Christ from the work of the Spirit is concerned, but that the topic was greatly clarified by John. Later theology very wisely took its cue from the Fourth Gospel.

It is notorious that Paul does not always distinguish between the ascended Christ and the Holy Spirit. We cannot even say that he totally identifies the two, since there are passages, such as Rom. 8.9–11, II Cor. 13.13, where he seems to distinguish the three 'Persons' clearly enough. On the other hand there are also passages where he seems virtually to identify them. One of these I shall be examining below, but another is the very much vexed passage II Cor. 3.16–17. In my article already referred to in Chapter 4, I have concluded that Ingo Hermann is right when he says that we have here an 'economic' identification of the Son with the Spirit, that is, that they are identical as far as our experience is concerned, though they are to be distinguished as entities.[1] I have also suggested that in I Cor. 2.10–16, a passage very much concerned with the doctrine of the Spirit, Paul does not, in practice, distinguish between the risen Christ and the Spirit.[2]

But we are concerned with the topic of heavenly intercession: the crucial passage here is Rom. 8.26–36. Paul begins by saying that the Spirit intercedes for us, indeed he intercedes in us, since Paul seems to identify the unintelligible noises of glossolalia with the prayers of the Spirit:

> but the Spirit himself intercedes for us with sighs too deep for words. And he who searches the hearts of men knows what is the mind of the Spirit, because the Spirit intercedes for the saints according to the will of God (8.26–27).

Here 'he who searches the hearts' is of course God the Father, not Christ. We have thus a picture of the Spirit guiding or inspiring Christians to pray aright, even if their prayers are expressed in unintelligible language. At this point we seem to be on the subject simply of Christian prayer. Prayer is made in the Spirit to the Father.

A few verses further on Paul seems to have altered his theme slightly. He is now thinking of possible hostile forces: 'If God is for us, who is against us?' (v. 31). And verse 33 continues: 'Who is to bring any charge against God's elect? It is God who justifies; who is to condemn?' (vv. 33–34). The next sentence may be raising and discussing the possibility that Jesus Christ should condemn Christians, or else Paul is simply strongly affirming that Jesus Christ is the one who died and rose for us, and consequently we have nothing to fear. In the ensuing verses Paul mentions a whole series of adverse circumstances that Christians may have to endure (v. 35: 'tribulation, distress, persecution, etc.') and in verse 38 he gives a list of potentially adverse powers that could be regarded as bringing about these circumstances. So he does certainly have in mind the vindication of Christians from those who would attack them. But the point is that, in the course of reassuring his readers about possible dangers and disasters, he says of Jesus Christ: 'who died, who was raised from the dead, and who indeed intercedes for us' (v. 34). The word for 'intercedes' here is *entunchanei*, whereas that used of the Spirit in verse 26 is *huperentunchanei*. But there is no real difference of meaning between the two verbs: in verse 27 Paul uses *entunchanei* of the action of the Spirit and this is the verb which the author of Hebrews uses of the ascended Christ's perpetual intercession on behalf of Christians in Heb. 7.25. The suggestion that verses 26–27 refer to intercession on earth, whereas verse 34 refers to intercession in heaven, does not help. It would be a distinction without a difference.

Another passage in which Paul seems, by the standards of later theology at least, to confuse the function of the ascended Christ with the function of the Holy Spirit is II Cor. 1.20:

> For all the promises of God find their Yes in him (Christ). That is why we utter the Amen through him to the glory of God.

This might be merely a statement that our prayer is made 'Through Jesus Christ our Lord'. But it seems more likely that 'uttering the Amen' has a wider significance here. We utter the Amen to God's promises by acting on them, responding to them, living them out in our lives. Of course all this is summed up and consciously represented in Christian worship, which is certainly in mind here. But later theology would prefer to say that we live out the life of Christ in the power of the Holy Spirit, and that our worship is offered through Christ indeed, but in the Spirit.

So, we may safely conclude that Paul did not have a clearly worked out doctrine of heavenly intercession. He could equally say that Christ intercedes or the Spirit intercedes. As far as we know, he never applied his mind to distinguishing the function of Christ and the Spirit as far as intercession is concerned. In this respect later theology, under the influence of the Fourth Gospel, was more precise and found a more satisfactory doctrine of the Spirit.

Colossians does not seem to advance at all on Paul's position. There are very few references to the Spirit in the epistle.[3] On the other hand, the writer says in 1.28 that he desires to present every man perfect in Christ, which suggests that for him the ascended Christ performs all the functions that later theology ascribed to the Spirit. But Ephesians has rather more light to shed.[4] Apart from a number of passages which refer to the Spirit as the source or sphere of the Christian life, we have 1.3; 2.18; 2.22, in all of which we seem to have references to something like the heavenly intercession. In 1.3, the author says that 'the God and

Father of our Lord Jesus Christ has blessed us in Christ with every spiritual blessing in the heavenly places'. One of the features that distinguishes Ephesians from the genuine Paulines is its emphasis on already accomplished salvation. Christians already are in the heavenly places: here they inherit a spiritual blessing 'in Christ'. It may even indicate that the author of Ephesians had arrived at a doctrine of 'through Christ in the Spirit' which was to be that of traditional Christian theology. This impression is confirmed by 2.18, where the author writes: 'for through him (Christ) we both have access in one Spirit to the Father'. This is exactly the later doctrine. In 2.22 'in the Lord' and 'in the Spirit' seem to be absolutely parallel, but on the basis of 2.18 we are justified in reading the same scheme here as there. We may also note 4.30: 'do not grieve the Holy Spirit of God', which implies that the author held a very personal doctrine of the Spirit. One cannot grieve a thing or a force. Another peculiarity of Ephesians is that the author believed in the existence of a class of evil spirits (see 2.2; 6.12) which even seems to operate in the heavenly sphere. But we do gain the impression that the author of Ephesians is moving towards the Johannine position on the relation of the Spirit to the ascended Christ.

We now turn to the doctrine of the Spirit in the Epistle to the Hebrews, a somewhat complicated theme, since the author uses that word *pneuma* in five distinguishable senses, only one of which refers to the Holy Spirit. They are as follows: (1) The Holy Spirit (2) angels are spirits; e.g. 1.7,14 (3) human beings can be referred to as spirits, e.g. 12.9,23 (4) *pneuma* is part of man's make-up: see 3.12, the only instance of this use in Hebrews (5) *pneuma* is the substance of the divine nature; this is an interpretation of 9.14, which is discussed below.

As far as Hebrews' use of *pneuma* to mean the Holy Spirit is concerned, most occurrences of the word in this sense are quite straightforward. Thus the Holy Spirit speaks through the scriptures, a belief common to all Jews and early Christians; see 3.7; 9.8; 10.15. Then the Holy Spirit is the agent of miraculous or unusual human achievements, as in 2.4. With this we may put 6.4, where those who have been baptized and have progressed some way in the Christian life are described as having 'become partakers of the Holy Spirit'.

This leaves us with the only two passages about the Holy Spirit which could possibly have any reference to the heavenly intercession. The first is 10.29, where the author writes:

How much worse punishment do you think will be deserved by the man who has spurned the Son of God, and profaned the blood of the covenant by which he was sanctified, and outraged the Spirit of grace?

This passage is very like 6.4, where the author is also on the topic of apostasy. The reference is, of course, to the Holy Spirit. But it is not enough to remark, as Bruce does, that 'the Spirit of grace', means 'the gracious Spirit',[5] or to observe with Spicq that it means 'l'esprit d'amour qui fut si généreux à son égard'.[6] The passage has a definite messianic reference. Strathmann draws our attention to Zechariah 12.10:

And I will pour out on the house of David and the inhabitants of Jerusalem a spirit of compassion and supplication, so that, when they look on him whom they have pierced, they shall mourn for him as one mourns for an only child, and weep bitterly over him, as one weeps over a first-born.[7]

The LXX translates the Hebrew *ruaḥ ḥen* ('Spirit of compassion') with *pneuma charitos*, exactly the phrase used in Heb. 10.29. This verse was regarded as messianic in the early church. We find it quoted of the piercing of the dead Christ's side by the soldier in John 19.37, and of the parousia in Revelation 1.7. Hence 'the spirit of grace' in this context in Hebrews must mean the gift of the Holy Spirit whereby converts have been enabled to recognize the Messiah in Christ crucified. It seems to imply that the author is writing to Jewish Christians, since the verse in Zechariah would seem to be limited to them, and anyway it was Jews who caused the death of Christ. Windisch with great virtuosity quotes a parallel from what we now know as the Qumran documents but what in his day was restricted to the Zadokite document.[8] This reference to the Holy Spirit, therefore, contains great significance for the author of the Epistle to the Hebrews. As Montefiore well points out, it shows that he held a personal view of the Spirit: 'It is not possible to insult a thing, only a person.'[9] But it still does not suggest any activity in heaven, only on earth. As far as we have seen, the author believed in two divine beings, the Holy Spirit and the ascended Jesus. But only the latter operates in heaven.

There is, however, one ambiguous passage where some scholars see a reference to the Holy Spirit as involved in the process of salvation. This is 9.14:

> For if the sprinkling of defiled persons with the blood of goats and bulls and with the ashes of a heifer sanctifies for the purification of the flesh, how much more shall the blood of Christ, who through the eternal Spirit offered himself without blemish to God, purify your conscience from dead works to serve the living God?

The RSV prejudges the issue by rendering the Greek *dia pneumatos aiōniou* with 'through the eternal Spirit'. Strictly speaking it is a mistranslation since there is nothing in Greek corresponding to 'the'. If this is a reference to the Holy Spirit, then that Spirit is brought into the heavenly places by the author of the epistle, because he is integrally connected with Christ's offering of himself. But does the phrase refer to the Holy Spirit?

Of the twelve commentators whose works I have consulted only three think the phrase refers to the Holy Spirit. These are Wickham,[10] Strathmann, and Bruce. They all indicate in one way or another that it means that by the Holy Spirit Jesus was enabled to make his offering. Wickham comments: 'The words seem to take us into unfathomable depths of the Divine Nature', and Bruce admits that it is 'extremely difficult to interpret with satisfactory precision'. Otto Kuss, it should be added, is uncertain as to whether the phrase refers to Christ's being (*Sein*) or endowment (*Aufgabe*).[11]

The great majority of editors, however, refer the phrase to something else. Westcott takes it of Christ's own spirit, which was eternal because he was God.[12] He well compares 7.16 'by the power of an indestructible life'. He also remarks quite significantly *à propos* 10.29: 'It will be observed that the action of the Holy Spirit falls into the background in the Epistle from the characteristic view which is given of the priestly work of Christ.' This view is supported by Windisch, who describes Christ as 'Ein Wesen, das ewigen Geist hatte'[13]; by Spicq ('sa personalité même'), who explicitly rejects the idea that the Holy Spirit is referred to; by J. Héring[14] and, apparently by J. Moffatt and W. Manson.[15] It is also accepted by Montefiore who paraphrases 'in his eternal nature'. In fact this latter interpretation seems much the more likely. Nowhere else in his work does the author show any indications of a doctrine that would associate the Holy Spirit with Christ's entry into the heavenly realm. He does not use *aiōnios* of the Holy Spirit anywhere else. It seems much more likely that we have here the view that Christ, the pre-existent being, since he is by nature divine and immortal, could not be annihilated by death. We probably find the same doctrine in I Peter 3.18–19, where it seems likely that *en hō/i* ('in which') means *en hō/i pneumati* ('in which spirit').[16] It contrasts with the more primitive view, witnessed in Acts 13.35, that the Messiah had to appeal to God from the realm of death for salvation.

So, according to the Epistle to the Hebrews, there is no place for the Spirit in the task of heavenly intercession. All is done by the ascended Christ. This is clear enough, and we cannot accuse the author of the Epistle of obscurity on this point. However, when we try to make sense of his christology in the light of his doctrine of Christ as the heavenly intercessor, we find ourselves in very great difficulties indeed. Hebrews presents us with a picture of a divine pre-existent being, whom perhaps he thought of as Lord, though he also calls him *apaugasma* and *charaktēr* (1.3). This being became a man Jesus Christ in the mode of sonship. He was a fully human being, since he was subject to emotion, learned obedience through suffering, and prayed with strong tears and crying to the Father to be saved from (eternal) death. In response to his prayer the Father raised him from the dead, and he now remains in heaven, continually making intercession for us on the basis of his one perfect offering of himself. He still retains, it seems, some of his human characteristics since he can sympathize with our infirmities, having been tempted, though sinless. He can also have communication with us, since he is described as our shepherd (13.20).

The author of Hebrews nowhere faced the question of the 'glorified humanity', just as he does not face the question of how the *apaugasma* could have become a man. We have seen from 9.14 that there is a hint of a doctrine of the Lord's eternal divinity. How is this compatible with having prayed to be saved from death? (or from the fear of death, if that is how you interpret 5.7). He does not even tell us whether the divine being carried his humanity into heaven with him. Hebrews has therefore presented a christology which seems straightforward only because he does not face any of its problems. He may have been aware of them, or he may simply never have thought through his christology sufficiently to come into contact with them. But in fact, as far as the heavenly intercession is concerned, he is less help than Paul. Paul does at least bring in the Holy Spirit as an intercessor, even though he is ambiguous about the relation of the Spirit to the ascended Christ.

Hebrews does not make use of the Holy Spirit at all in this area, and his doctrine suffers in consequence. One cannot altogether suppress a suspicion that, in the mind of the author of Hebrews, Christ may have occupied a position analogous to that of Philo's Logos: he is both God and man, or rather now God and now man and now God again. Not that the author of Hebrews was an Arian two hundred and fifty years before Arius, but that the implications of his christology would have worked out in the direction of Arianism. At any rate the ascended Christ in the Epistle to the Hebrews is burdened with functions which makes better sense to attribute to the Holy Spirit, if indeed they are necessary at all.

In the Fourth Gospel it seems as if this problem has been worked out: it is not that the Paraclete takes over the rôle of heavenly intercessor. It is rather that there does not seem to be any need for intercession in heaven. There is no lack of references either to Jesus praying, or to the disciples praying in Jesus' name. But, with one exception, Jesus only prays while on earth. Thus he prays at the feeding of the five thousand (6.11), he prays at the raising of Lazarus (11.41–42), and he prays at the point where John is probably giving us his version of Gethsemane (12.27–28). Finally he utters his great high-priestly prayer, the whole of chapter 17. However different these examples of prayer may be from what we learn of Jesus' prayers in the synoptic gospels, they are presented as examples of prayer. The one remarkable exception to this occurs in 14.16–17: 'And I will pray the Father, and he will give you another counsellor to be with you forever, even the Spirit of truth'. This may be regarded as unique, since it refers to the sending of the Holy Spirit, an event which we know from 7.39 cannot take place until Jesus has been glorified.

The function of the Paraclete is not to pray, but to teach and to represent Christ. Not that he is a surrogate for an absent Lord; 15.1f. alone would rule out any such suggestion. But he enables the disciples to understand the full significance of Jesus (see 14.16–17,26; 15.25–26). In 16.7f. we are told that the sending of the Paraclete will benefit the disciples. This is no doubt primarily because he will enable the disciples to understand fully the Christ event – or perhaps we should say the coming of the Logos. But it is also because his coming will solve the problem of the bodily presence of the risen Lord. In Chapter 4 we reached the conclusion that John did not have a doctrine of the 'glorified humanity' of the risen Lord existing somewhere in heaven. His doctrine of the Paraclete made this unnecessary. There is no suggestion of the two functions clashing, as in Paul. The Son remains in heaven in the state which he occupied originally from all eternity, with the Father (17.24). He can be known by faith to the faithful. But this knowledge must be 'in the Spirit', since we have the repeated assertion that the Spirit will teach the disciples about Christ (see especially 16.12–15).

As for prayer after the resurrection of Christ, this is to be done in Christ's name: in 14.13–14 Christ promises to do anything that the disciples ask in his name. This is not a doctrine of Christ as the eternal intercessor in heaven, such as we find in Hebrews. Perhaps 15.16 is a little nearer this: 'Whatever you ask the Father in my name, he may give it to you.' But the 'name of Christ' means 'the Spirit of Christ' when analysed, and the immediate reference is to the disciples bearing much fruit, so the implication seems to be that, if they bring forth the fruit of the Spirit, they will be able to pray in the Spirit. This is rather supported by 16.23–24:

In that day you will ask nothing of me. Truly, truly I say to you, if you ask anything of the Father, he will give it to you in my name. Hitherto you have asked nothing in my name; ask, and you will receive, that your joy may be full.

The words 'in that day' refer to the period after the resurrection. And 'hitherto' also suggests the beginning of a new period. John seems to be suggesting that the disciples will have direct access to the Father. But this will be the period of the Spirit, after Jesus has been glorified. It seems, therefore, very likely indeed that John is speaking of the disciples praying in the Spirit through the Lord Jesus, as they no doubt did in the church of his day. The ensuing verses, 16.26–28, confirm this impression. Jesus explicitly disavows an intercessory rôle: 'In that day you will ask in my name; and I do not say to you that I shall pray the Father for you; for the Father himself loves you, because you have loved me and have believed that I came forth from the Father.' The disciples will have direct access to the Father, but it is impossible to believe that in John's view this can take place apart from the Spirit.

No doubt he omits a direct reference to the Spirit because he is still preserving some semblance of historical verisimilitude.

The same impression is conveyed by Christ's words in the great high-priestly prayer: in 17.17 he prays for the disciples: 'Sanctify them in the truth; thy word is truth', and in 17.19 he prays 'that they may be consecrated in the truth'. There seems to be no good reason why the RSV should have translated the Greek verb *hagiazō* which occurs three times in these three verses 17–19 with two different English words. In its context it is very difficult not to connect it with the work of the Holy Spirit, the sanctifier, who is after all the Spirit of truth.

Thus in the question of the heavenly intercession John has shown himself to be a deeper theologian than either Paul or the author of Hebrews, perhaps because he wrote at a greater distance in time from the crucial events. He does not attempt a doctrine of a 'glorified humanity'. He does not confuse the function of the ascended Christ with that of the Holy Spirit. He sees no need for a doctrine of Christ as our intercessor with the Father. Christians can approach God through the Son in the Spirit. Just because the Word is God and is always with God John does not need a doctrine of a divine, or semi-divine, mediator whose function it is to present our case to the Father. The Word reveals and saves. He does not plead.

The doctrine of the intercessory activity of the ascended Christ has taken two forms in the history of the church, a more extreme and a milder. The more extreme form consists in saying that Christ in heaven constantly propitiates the Father's wrath by virtue of his one great sacrifice which he continually pleads before the Father's face. This is *not* the doctrine of the Epistle to the Hebrews; no words corresponding to 'propitiation' occur in that work, and in one place where the author could have identified Jesus with the scape-goat on the Day of Atonement, he pointedly refrains from doing so (13.10–13). Nor, I believe, is this Pauline doctrine. This may seem a surprising claim, since Paul does use what looks like the language of propitiation; e.g. *hilastērion* (RSV 'expiation') in Rom. 3.25. But I believe that in all such passages Paul is in fact teaching, not that Christ propitiated the Father, but that the Father vindicated Christ when he was accused and killed by the powers of evil, and that we are vindicated in him. We have already seen a hint of this above in our discussion of Rom. 8.34.[17]

There are, however, hints of this doctrine of propitiation in some parts of the New Testament. One such passage is I John 2.1–2:

> If anyone does sin, we have an advocate with the Father, Jesus Christ
> the righteous; and he is the expiation for our sins.

The Greek word rendered 'expiation' is *hilasmos*. It is very significant
that the author of I John uses the title 'Paraclete' (here translated
'advocate') for Jesus, not for the Holy Spirit. I believe that Raymond
Brown is right in his suggestion that this is an instance of the author of
I John reverting to an earlier and cruder type of theology.[18] Certainly
there is no such doctrine in the Fourth Gospel.

A similar theology seems to be implicit in the use of the word *mesitēs*
('mediator') in I Timothy 2.5: 'there is one mediator between God and
men, the man Jesus Christ'. I have suggested elsewhere that this phrase
goes back ultimately to the use of *mesitēs* in the LXX version of Job
9.33.[19] Paul in his authentic letters never uses *mesitēs* of Christ; indeed
he explicitly repudiates the word in Galatians 3.19–20, where the
presence of a mediator shows the inferiority of the old covenant. The
word is used by Hebrews of Jesus, where he is called a mediator of the
new covenant (Heb. 8.6; 9.15; 12.24). The fact that Jesus is not called
a mediator absolutely is important, and in any case we have suggested
that Hebrews' doctrine of the heavenly activity of Christ is unsatisfactory. The truth is that, if the word 'mediator' is to have its obvious
meaning, a mediator between God and man must be neither God nor
man, or at least neither completely God nor completely man. This is
exactly the position of Philo's Logos, witness this passage:

> To his Word, his chief messenger, highest in use and honour, the
> Father of all has given the special prerogative of standing on the
> border and separating the creature from the creator. This same Word
> both pleads with the Immortal as suppliant for afflicted mortality,
> and acts as ambassador for the ruler to the subject. He glories in this
> prerogative, and proudly describes it in these words 'and I stood
> between the Lord and you', that is, neither uncreated as God, nor
> created as you, but mid-way between the two extremes.[20]

Thus ontologically a true mediator cannot be either truly God or truly
man, precisely the nature of Arius' Logos. Soteriologically also a
mediator would seem to imply that in some way God is to be acted

upon or persuaded. Certainly the mediator for whom Job longed was to be someone who could arbitrate between God and man, which suggests that some sort of an arrangement could be arrived at whereby God should be induced either to abandon, or at least to modify, his demands upon men.

This doubtful use of the conception of mediatorship may be illustrated by a passage from J. K. Mozley. It runs as follows: 'The situation produced by sin lies, as it were, between God and men. Therefore the intervention of Christ is his mediation between God and man. Christ's relation to God and to man may affect the character of that mediation; his intervention may be interpreted (not rightly, I think, but still possibly) as operative upon man alone, and not upon God; nevertheless the result of that intervention is that the situation as between God and man changes. It changes not through direct dealing of God and man with one another, but through the action of Christ. Christ is a third to God and man, though he is both God and man, for he is neither simply God nor simply man.'[21] Later Mozley explicitly commits himself to the view that Christ effected a change in God. 'And that which he has done he did first unto God.'[22] A similar desire to seek for a mediator who can somehow stand outside God and man is evinced in the tendency in one tradition of Roman Catholic and Orthodox theology to describe the Blessed Virgin Mary as 'Mediatrix'. In 1891 Pope Leo XIII described her as 'mediatrix to the Mediator'.[23] Indeed some Orthodox theology goes beyond this, elevating her very much to the position of Philo's Logos. Lossky quotes with approval St Gregory Palamas' sentence describing the Blessed Virgin as 'the boundary of created and uncreated nature'.[24]

This is, at any rate, the form in which the doctrine of the heavenly intercession has often been expressed in traditional theology. Thus Leo the Great writes: 'in the same flesh which he took from the virgin he carries on the propitiation';[25] and a sermon attributed to John Chrysostom claims that whenever God is disposed to punish men for their sins 'seeing the sinless humanity at his right hand, he is placated'.[26] A modern upholder of this tradition is undoubtedly Karl Barth: In his *Doctrine of the Word of God* in the *Church Dogmatics* volumes I, 1 and I, 2 he gives the impression that he is defending a doctrine of non-penal substitution but in volume II, 1 he declares himself without any ambiguity: 'Christ has borne the wrath of God against those who are enemies of his grace. . . . He has borne the punishment which was rightly ours.' And again much later on he writes: 'But he could only bear it because he was God: no mere creature could bear the burden of the eternal wrath of God against sin', and he goes on to say that because Christ bore it we need not bear it.[27] Compare also O. C. Quick: 'In that utterance ("My God, my God, why hast thou forsaken me?") is recorded the true penalty of sin which the Son of God alone could have the strength to bear without perishing eternally.'[28] All such expressions of the atoning work of Christ encounter the same fundamental objection: they imply that Christ's task was, and is, to act upon the Father, to induce him to change his mind, to function as a moderator to his original intransigence. This is not in accordance with the main drive of the theology of the New Testament which claims rather that God in Christ has acted for our redemption, has declared his goodwill towards us. There is therefore no need for a continuing ministry of propitiation, which suggests in any case a fatal dichotomy between the Father and the Son, leading in terms of christology to a doctrine whereby the Son cannot be of the same status with the Father, since he has to compromise himself by adopting some form of human nature. And in soteriological terms it puts all the burden of maintaining justice on the Father and all the element of love with the Son. Inevitably we are faced with a doctrine of some sort of heavenly transaction between the Father and the Son. But modern theology is rightly suspicious of any doctrine of heavenly transactions.

The milder version of this doctrine takes the form of saying, not that Christ exercises a ministry of propitiation, but rather one of intercession. He continually intercedes with the Father for us. This is sometimes put in the form that Christ, having privileged access to the Father, is obviously the best person to whom to entrust our petitions. He knows the best way, and perhaps the best moment, for our requests to be preferred to the Father. In Catholic Christianity, both Roman and Orthodox, the same ministry is often attributed to the Blessed Virgin Mary. Christ in this scheme is put on the side of God, and it is the mother of God (as she is called) who is in the best position to present our requests. The great champion of this approach is S. Alphonsus Liguori, who suggests that Mary may inspire us with more confidence than does Jesus, of whom we may be somewhat afraid. But essentially the same view can be paralleled among some modern Catholics, both

Orthodox and Roman. Thus Lossky writes: 'She [Mary] obtains eternal benefits. . . . No gift is received in the Church without the assistance of the Mother of God'.[29] Leo XIII described her as 'dispenser of all graces' and 'advocate'.[30] His predecessor Pius IX was even more specific: 'It is God's will that we should receive everything through Mary.' And 'what she asks she obtains. Her supplications (*Einsprüche*) can never go unheard'.[31] Finally I refer to another Orthodox writer, Evdokimov. Under the heading 'the mariological aspect of the Church' he writes: 'Although the Word, in his objective relationship, considered in himself is all-sufficient, the insufficiency is in us and we have need of the maternal protection, we have need to find ourselves as children on the knees of the Church in order to read the Word.' He appears to be alluding to our need for St Mary's intercession.[32] A little later on he writes that 'she represents the ministry of prayer . . . [she] presents the prayer of the Church'. Quite recently when the Pope visited the little town of Knock in the west of Ireland I heard this point of view expressed on British television by someone who was defending the Roman Catholic practice of asking the Blessed Virgin to pray for us. Her Son, it was claimed, could not refuse her anything, so if only we can persuade her to present our prayers to him, we can be sure that they will reach God the Father with the best possible recommendations. What all these quotations have in common is a distrust of the mercy of God and the salvation revealed and activated in Christ. Whether we regard Christ or Mary as our intercessor with God, we betray a doubt as to the reality of God's goodwill towards us.

The doctrine of the glorified humanity of the Son plays its part also in this form of the doctrine of the heavenly intercession. Indeed in the Epistle to the Hebrews itself we can see this taking place, for we are told that 'we have not a high priest who is unable to sympathise with our weaknesses, but one who in every respect has been tempted as we are, yet without sinning' (Heb. 4.15).

Whether this doctrine is expressed in the form of the Son's intercessory activity with the Father, or in the form of the intercessory activity of the Blessed Virgin with Christ, it is not one which can be easily defended on rational grounds. The latter form is really a very refined form of paganism. It suggests that God needs to be approached as if he was an oriental monarch who has his favourites, or who at least is better approached by some members of his court than by others, or even better approached when he is in a good mood, a piece of information only available of course to those who are specially intimate with him. Or, to put it in more modern terms, he is like some very lofty bureaucrat. If we approach him directly our petition will go through the usual channels, be dealt with by subordinates, and only reach him, if at all, after an interminable delay. But if we can find a personal friend of his to present our request for us, he can go directly to the great man and have it dealt with immediately.

Even in the more refined form, as presented, for example, in the Epistle to the Hebrews, it is doubtful if this doctrine of the Son's intercessory work with the Father is satisfactory. Christ at least, the argument runs, knows what it is to be man. He at least knows our predicament from personal experience. The unavoidable corollary is that God the Father lacks such experience and depends on the Son for obtaining it. It implies that the incarnation was, among other things, a fact-finding mission. But this seems to defeat one of the ultimate reasons for working out a christology. The only reason we are interested in explaining the significance of Jesus is that we believe that in him God was in Christ reconciling the world to himself. The writers of the New Testament and the earliest Christians did not imagine God as somehow being deficient in full information about our human condition. The Old Testament is full of assurances that God knows us better than we know ourselves (e.g. Ps. 139; Isa. 49.16). So we do not need to worry about whether God really understands our condition. We do not need, and should not seek, a mediator in that sense. What the incarnation has added to what we can know of God from the finest insights of the Old Testament is that God (not just Christ) is so fully concerned for our good that he is willing to go to the utmost lengths conceivable to rescue us and bring us back to himself. If we construct a doctrine of Christ continually interceding for us in heaven we have modified that original and essential insight. It is, after all, not God the Father, but Christ who knows our condition. Even if we also qualify Christ as God the Son, we have not remedied the primary error. The New Testament claims that God was in Christ reconciling the world to himself. The doctrine of Christ's heavenly intercession suggests that only one part of God was concerned in this reconciliation.

The conception of Jesus' glorified humanity still continuing somehow in heaven plays an essential part in this doctrine of Christ's heavenly intercession. It is true that the author of the Epistle to the Hebrews nowhere explicitly expresses such a doctrine, but it must be implied in his christology, since he claims that because of his humanity Christ is peculiarly well qualified to intercede for us. Those who defend such a doctrine today are, therefore, obliged to explain how we can continue to claim that Jesus' humanity affects the destiny of believers or is integrally connected with the contemporary process of redemption. We have already noted the difficulties into which the Reformers ran when they tried to retain a doctrine of the persistence of Christ's body in heaven. Luther committed himself to the extraordinarily difficult claim that Christ's intercession with the Father is '*oralis et realis*' (oral and real). Calvin very understandably jibbed at this, and was content to say that it was '*realis*'.[33] But even this is unsatisfactory. God does not pray. When we want to say, as we should, that God acting in us moves us to pray, we use the language of the Holy Spirit. Once again we seem to be driven to fall back on the well-tried formula, recommended by the use of the church 'through Christ in the Spirit'. The attempt to portray Christ as praying for us as well, in the way in which Hebrews does, is only to introduce an element of confusion.

It may be objected that our protest against the concept of heavenly transactions taking place between the Father and the Son is inconsistent with our accepting and defending a doctrine of the Trinity. When we claim that, on the basis of his revelation of himself in Jesus Christ, we must conclude that God is Three in One, are we not accepting the notion of a heavenly transaction, or at least of a heavenly construction? Not, I would claim, if we clearly understand why we believe that God is Trinity. This belief is an attempt to do justice to the magnitude and scope of the revelation, and also the redemption, which God has effected in Christ. At every point we can relate this doctrine to Christian experience: we do know God as Father; we do experience his redemption through his divine Word, in the form of Jesus Christ; we do acknowledge God's sanctifying work within us in the context of the church. Nowhere here are we compelled to assume any heavenly activities to which we are not a party. Nowhere do we suggest that something is happening within the Trinity independently of us. It is not an essential feature of the doctrine of the Trinity to claim that one part of God is acting upon another. The doctrine of the Trinity is a necessary attempt to do justice to what God has revealed himself in Jesus Christ to be. The doctrine of the heavenly intercession of Christ, and still more of his heavenly propitiation, is an attempt unjustifiably to insert humanity into the very being of God. Admittedly this is a feature of the traditional account of the person of Christ, but it is a feature which has caused great difficulties in working out the implications of christology, and it is not, I believe, essential to a doctrine concerning Jesus Christ which measures up to the scope of what the New Testament says about him.

Have we left ourselves any room for a doctrine of the priesthood of Christ? This is a doctrine which is certainly found in the New Testament and not only in the Epistle to the Hebrews. There is a sense in which the whole of the New Testament record is an attempt to explain how God in Christ has shown himself to be our priest. He has revealed himself and activated his love for us in Jesus Christ. It is surely significant that in the eighth chapter of Romans, discussed earlier in this chapter, Paul associates Christ's praying for us with his work on our behalf, and that work in Paul's theology is unmistakably the work of God. In other words, the nearer Paul came to describing Christ as God, the farther he was from regarding him as an intermediate power who can give us privileged access to God. If Paul had been able to distinguish more clearly the function of Christ from that of the Spirit, as John was able to do later, he would not perhaps have suggested that Christ intercedes on our behalf.

But finally, I should try to give some account of how I understand the priesthood of Christ. To begin with, he is our priest in that he alone presented a wholly obedient life to God. He did this on our behalf in the sense in which I have explained the matter in the last chapter. He is therefore also our priest in that he provides us with a model of what our humanity is intended by God to be. In this sense he represents us, since he has provided the representative model of humanity. This is connected with the historical intention of Jesus himself, since I believe that good grounds can be shown for believing that Jesus did see himself as offering a representative sacrifice by means of his death. This priesthood is carried on, very imperfectly, by the church, and therefore links up, in the way, already considered, with a satisfactory doctrine of the body of Christ. But we need a doctrine of the Spirit to make sense of this. If we attempt a doctrine of Christ's priesthood without a satisfactory doctrine of the Holy Spirit, we are in danger of isolating

Christ, casting him in the rôle of an intermediate being who acts upon God on our behalf, and end up by presenting an account of a heavenly transaction.

We can and should offer our prayers 'through Jesus Christ our Lord' in the sense that we offer them through the divine Word known to us in the form or image of Jesus Christ. This means both that we offer them on the basis of what God has revealed of himself in Jesus Christ, and that we approach God in the Spirit through the Word or Son, whom we know in the form of Jesus Christ. This is, we may say, the priesthood of God in Christ. This priesthood is to be exercised through the activity of the church in the world, and it is only on this basis that we can justify the continuance of an order of ordained priests in the ministry of the church. God in Christ appeals to all men to be reconciled to him in Christ. This ministry of reconciliation he entrusts to the church (see II Cor. 5.19–6.2). There is, therefore, a priesthood of God in Christ by means of the Spirit. And this priesthood is exercised through the church. In this respect we can say that the church on behalf of God-in-Christ has a priesthood which is directed towards the whole world.

This account still leaves ample room for the worship of God and a ministry of intercession, both carried on by the church. Indeed we have no reason to confine either of these activities to the church on earth. The one point about the life of the departed in heaven on which we have clear testimony in the New Testament is that they worship God and pray. But here too we must maintain the invaluable formula: 'through Jesus Christ in the Spirit'. We mean by this exactly the same as we mean when we say: 'through the divine Word known in the form of Jesus Christ in the Spirit' or even 'through the Son in the Spirit', as long as it is understood that this does not necessarily imply an identity between Jesus' sonship when on earth and the eternal relation between the first and second 'Persons' of the Trinity. We make our intercessions to God through the Word in the Spirit not because God needs to be informed about our human condition, but because God is our Father, and it is natural that we make our wants known to him. Indeed, we have the highest authority for saying that he wishes us to make our wants known to him. We make our prayers through the Word known in the form of Jesus Christ because that is the mode in which God has supremely revealed himself. We do so in the Spirit, because experience teaches us that this is the effect of God's approach to us in Jesus Christ if we respond in faith.

Nor does this approach by-pass the scheme set forth in the Epistle to the Hebrews whereby Jesus Christ made the one great sacrifice on the basis of which believers can now approach God. That one great sacrifice is one way of expressing the action of God in Jesus Christ as he came to reveal himself supremely and redeem mankind. What I do repudiate is the notion, not by any means necessarily implied in Hebrews, that that sacrifice somehow continues to work on God, rendering favourable to us a God who would otherwise be hostile. I do not, of course, follow the author of the Epistle to the Hebrews in representing Christ as eternally interceding for us with the Father: I have explained above why I think it more satisfactory to say that we intercede in the Holy Spirit.

This leaves one question to be faced. I have said that the saints in heaven pray. How then can we possibly deny that Jesus himself, the king of saints, prays for his followers? I would not attempt to do so. But I must add that, like us, he prays through the Word, in the Spirit. Should we not then ask him to pray for us, in the same way that Catholic Christians from early times have asked the saints, and notably the Blessed Virgin Mary, to pray for them? The answer to this question will depend on the tradition to which the answerer belongs. Those who have been accustomed to ask for the prayers of the saints will of course ask Jesus for his prayers. Those who have not, probably will not. I hope it is a practice that can be left to the decision of the individual Christian, and not something that will be regarded as either obligatory or prohibited. The important point is that, since the coming of Jesus Christ, all our prayer is made 'through Jesus Christ in the Spirit', and also that, however we pray, we do not let our prayers degenerate into a situation in which we ask anyone, whether God the Word, Jesus Christ, or St Mary, to exercise a special influence with God on our behalf. Since the coming of Jesus Christ we do not need, and should not attempt, to use any method of bringing God round to our side. In Jesus Christ he has declared that he is on our side already.

As an envoi to this work I have only two remarks to make. The first is the observation that what set out to be an essay on the place of the risen Christ in the life of the Christian has turned out to be very much a book about the activity of the Holy Spirit. This is exactly as it should be and is to be regarded as an indication that the aim behind the writing of this book has not been wholly frustrated.

The second remark is a reminder about something with which I began. This book is an example of *fides quaerens intellectum*. There is a growing danger at the present moment that some church authorities and some of those responsible for popular Christian literature may succeed in conveying the impression that a group of radical theologians is irresponsibly attempting to subvert and remove doctrinal formulations which are still perfectly valid today, if only people would leave them alone. Shortly before writing this paragraph I heard an interview on BBC radio with Edward Schillebeeckx in which he asserted that his discussions with his inquisitors in Rome, though very cordial, were not even up to the theological level which he would expect in a discussion on a doctoral thesis. And only today in the catalogue of a well-known second-hand bookseller who prides himself on providing theological comment on his wares, I read a number of disparaging remarks about Karl Rahner, Edward Schillebeeckx and Hans Küng, as if they were rarefied intellectuals who enjoyed making things unnecessarily difficult for simple Christians. Most of those who disparage what they call 'radical' theology simply do not understand the relevant issues. No one has the right to sneer at such theologians (whether they deserve the epithet 'radical' is another question) who has not faced the problems of christology in the last quarter of the twentieth century in the West, and at least made some attempt to solve them.

The account of the risen Christ put forth in this work is not orthodox by the criterion of traditional christology. I have tried to explain why I cannot accept the account of the matter which traditional christology presents. But my alternative account is not intended to be a challenge or a defiance to orthodox believers. Let them continue to accept the orthodox christology by all means, as long as they are aware of why some of us, who have no penchant for heresy or schism, cannot accept it. And I hope that they will accept such an alternative account as mine as bearing at least the intention to think with the Catholic Church as far as intellectual integrity allows us.

NOTES

1. The Contemporary Debate

1. J. Moltmann, *The Crucified God*, ET London 1974.
2. J. Sobrino, *Christology at the Crossroads*, ET London 1978.
3. P. Gisel, *Vérité et Histoire: La Théologie dans le Modernité: Ernst Käsemann*, Paris, 1975.
4. Gisel, op. cit., pp. 142–3, 173, 177–8.
5. Ibid., pp. 291, 356, 394, 550.
6. Ibid., pp. 339, 329.
7. Ibid., p. 512.
8. Ibid., pp. 552–3.
9. Ibid., pp. 515–16, 509, 518–19, 535.
10. Ibid., pp. 497, 557.
11. Cf. ibid., p. 569, where Gisel describes Käsemann's theology as 'non-théiste'.
12. M. F. Wiles, *The Remaking of Christian Doctrine*, London 1974.
13. Wiles, op. cit., p. 51.
14. Ibid., p. 45.
15. Ibid., p. 48.
16. Ibid., p. 54.
17. Ibid., p. 53.
18. W. Kasper, *Jesus the Christ*, ET London 1976, p. 239.
19. See K. Rahner, *Theological Investigations* 1, ET London 1961, p. 162.
20. See A. T. Hanson, *Grace and Truth*, London 1975, pp. 167–8.
21. K. Rahner, *Foundations of Christian Faith*, ET London 1978.
22. Rahner, op. cit., pp. 174–5.
23. Ibid., p. 195.
24. Ibid., pp. 196–7.
25. Ibid., p. 199.
26. Ibid., p. 202.
27. Ibid., p. 215.
28. Ibid., p. 218.
29. Ibid., pp. 218–19.
30. Ibid., p. 224.
31. Ibid., p. 249.
32. Ibid., p. 290.
33. Ibid., p. 292.
34. Ibid., pp. 303–4.
35. E. Schillebeeckx, *Jesus: An Experiment in Christology*, ET London 1979; *Christ: The Christian Experience in the Modern World*, ET London 1980.

36. Schillebeeckx, *Jesus*, p. 295.
37. Ibid., p. 483.
38. Ibid., p. 571.
39. Ibid., p. 656.
40. Ibid., p. 653.
41. Ibid., p. 655.
42. Ibid., p. 658.
43. Ibid., p. 660.
44. Ibid., p. 661.
45. Ibid., p. 666.
46. Ibid., p. 669.
47. P. Hebblethwaite, *The New Inquisition? Schillebeeckx and Küng*, London 1980, pp. 143–4.
48. Schillebeeckx, *Christ*, p. 796.
49. Ibid., p. 832.
50. P. Hebblethwaite, 'The Appeal to Experience in Christology', in S. W. Sykes and J. P. Clayton (eds), *Christ, Faith and History*, Cambridge 1972, pp. 263–78.
51. Hebblethwaite, art. cit., p. 264.
52. Ibid., p. 269.
53. Ibid., p. 277.
54. B. Hebblethwaite, 'Incarnation – the Essence of Christianity?', *Theology*, March 1977, pp. 85–91.
55. Ibid., p. 85.
56. Ibid., p. 87.
57. Ibid., p. 88.
58. Ibid., p. 90.
59. Ibid., p. 91.
60. M. Goulder (ed.), *Incarnation and Myth: The Debate Continued*, London 1979.
61. *Incarnation and Myth*, p. 27.
62. Ibid., p. 28.
63. Ibid., p. 90.
64. It does not occur in Lampe's lexicon – G. W. H. Lampe (ed.), *A Patristic Greek Lexicon*, Oxford 1961.
65. Hebblethwaite, 'The Propriety of the Doctrine of the Incarnation as a Way of Interpreting Christ', *Scottish Journal of Theology*, vol. 33, no. 3, 1980, pp. 201–22.
66. See below p. 44.
67. W. N. Pittenger, *The Word Incarnate*, London 1959.

2. *The Traditional Doctrine of the Risen Christ*

1. J. Rivière, *The Doctrine of the Atonement*, ET 1909, I, p. 183.
2. H. E. W. Turner, *The Patristic Doctrine of Redemption*, London 1952, p. 121.

3. Tertullian, *De Resurrectione*, 51, quoted by J. G. Davies, *He Ascended into Heaven*, London 1958, p. 83.

4. Hippolytus, *Contra Noetum* 4, quoted by Davies, op. cit., p. 87.

5. Davies, op. cit., p. 121.

6. Ibid., pp. 128–9.

7. Ibid., p. 92.

8. Translated in Ps. CXXXVIII, 22, cited by Davies, op. cit., p. 102.

9. A. J. Tait, *The Heavenly Session of Our Lord*, London 1912, p. 64.

10. Tait, op. cit., p. 87.

11. Ibid., p. 92. He is quoting Cassian, *De Incarn*, 3.3. I have altered some of Tait's capitals and have corrected his punctuation. For the ensuing reference in Athanasius see J. P. Migne, *Patrologia Graeca*, vol. 26, Paris 1889. For the translation, see *The Orations of St Athanasius against the Arians*, in the Ancient and Modern Library of Modern Literature, London nineteenth century n.d., in loc.

12. E. Klostermann (ed.), Eusebius, *Contra Marcellum*, vol. IV, Berlin 1972, I, 1, 22, 23(b), my translation throughout.

13. W. Jaeger and H. Langerbeck (eds), *Gregorii Nysseni Sermones*, Pars Prior, vol. IX, Leiden 1967, 293, 616–7M; my translation throughout.

14. Ibid., 304, 627M.

15. Ibid.; E. Gebhardt (ed.), *In Ascensionem Christi*, 326, 693M.

16. R. M. Hübner, *Die Einheit des Leibes Christi bei Gregor von Nyssa*, Leiden 1974, pp. 46, 52–3.

17. Ibid., p. 95, my translation.

18. Ibid., p. 128.

19. Ibid., p. 206.

20. J. P. Migne (ed.), *Patrologia Graeca*, 44, Gregorii Nysseni, *Opera quae Reperi Potuerunt Omnia*, Paris 1863, 1320D, my translation.

21. Jaeger, op. cit., III, I, 222, 25–7.

22. Hübner, op. cit., p. 228.

23. Ibid., p. 103.

24. Ibid., p. 327, my translation.

25. Darwell Stone, *A History of the Doctrine of the Holy Eucharist*, vol. I, London 1909, pp. 97–8. Jerome is commenting on Eph. 1.7.

26. Stone, op. cit., vol. I, pp. 99–101.

27. Augustine, *De Fide et Symbolo* 6, cited by Davies, op. cit., pp. 139–40.

28. *De Symb.*, *Sermo ad Cat.* 3.7; quoted by Tait, op. cit., p. 66, in Latin; my translation.

29. See Tait, op. cit., p. 178.

30. *Ep. 187 ad Dardanum*, cited in Tait, p. 179.

31. See G. Martelet, *The Risen Christ and the Eucharistic World*, ET London 1976, p. 124.

32. Augustine, *Ep. 187*.

33. Margaret Miles, *Augustine on the Body*, Missoula, Montana 1979.

34. Miles, op. cit., pp. 108, 110.

35. Ibid., pp. 111–19.
36. Chrysostom, *In Ascens.* C3, cited by Tait, op. cit., p. 63.
37. S. D. F. Salmond (ed.), *John of Damascus* in *Post-Nicene Fathers*, vol. IX, *Exposition of the Orthodox Faith*, III, 3, 48.
38. Tait, op. cit., p. 182.
39. *Homily*, II, 9, cited in Davies, op. cit., pp. 158–9.
40. His discussion of the subject is to be found in *Summa Theologiae* IV, *Tertia Pars* 432–66, ed. Fratres Ordinis Praedicatorum, Madrid 1958; my translation from the Latin.
41. Ibid., 432–3.
42. Ibid., 434–5.
43. Ibid., 436–7.
44. Ibid., 453.
45. Ibid., 454.
46. Ibid., 462.
47. Ibid., 464–5.
48. Quoted in Tait, op. cit., p. 150.
49. Tait, p. 186.
50. J. Moltmann, *The Church in the Power of the Spirit*, ET London 1977, p. 253.
51. See Martelet, *The Risen Christ and the Eucharistic World*, p. 144; Calvin, *Institutes*, IV, xvii, 28, is quoting.
52. Tait, op. cit., p. 194.
53. See Tait, op. cit., pp. 188, 190, 200.
54. Ibid., p. 171.
55. Quoted by Stone, op. cit., vol. II, p. 530.
56. Ibid., p. 542.
57. B. F. Westcott, *The Revelation of the Risen Lord*, fourth ed., London 1887, pp. 68, 180, 181.
58. H. B. Swete, *The Ascended Christ*, London 1910, pp. 9–10. As with Tait, I have removed many of his capitals.
59. Swete, op. cit., pp. 27–8.
60. Ibid., p. 29.
61. Ibid., p. 92.
62. Ibid., p. 9.
63. Tait, op. cit., p. 210.
64. See ibid., p. 222.
65. Stone, op. cit., vol. II, p. 593.
66. Ibid., pp. 587f.
67. Davies, op. cit., p. 173; here too I have removed a number of capitals.
68. G. Kittel, *TWNT*, vol. VII, Stuttgart 1964. This article has been published in English under the title *The Church as the Body of Christ*, London 1965.
69. Davies, op. cit., p. 179.
70. Ibid., p. 180.

71. See above p. 26.
72. Tait, op. cit., p. 92.
73. Davies, op. cit., pp. 180–1.
74. Karl Barth, *Church Dogmatics*, ET Edinburgh 1960.
75. Barth, *Church Dogmatics*, IV, 2, p. 52.
76. Barth, *CD*, IV, 2, p. 63. This point of view of Augustine's was brought out during his controversy with Pelagius: see A. Harnack, *Outlines of the History of Dogma*, ET London 1893, pp. 352, 379. See also E. Teselle, *Augustine the Theologian*, London 1970, pp. 336–7.
77. *CD*, IV, 2, p. 49.
78. *CD*, III, 2, p. 464.
79. See III, 2, pp. 483 and 484.
80. See IV, 2, pp. 33f.
81. See also E. Jüngel, *The Doctrine of the Trinity*, Edinburgh 1976, p. 84.
82. *CD*, III, 2, p. 449.
83. *CD*, IV, 2, p. 145.
84. Ibid.
85. III, 2, p. 327.
86. Ibid., p. 448.
87. Ibid., pp. 454, 467.
88. IV, 2, p. 100.
89. Ibid., pp. 153, 349.
90. Ibid., p. 60.
91. III, 2, p. 334.
92. Ibid., p. 337.
93. IV, 2, p. 100.
94. Ibid., p. 28.
95. Ibid., p. 72.
96. Martelet, op. cit., pp. 83, 94.
97. Ibid., pp. 88–9.
98. Ibid., p. 125.
99. Ibid., p. 127.
100. Ibid., p. 136.
101. Stone, op. cit., vol. 2, p. 440.
102. Martelet, op. cit., pp. 145–6.
103. C. F. D. Moule, *The Origin of Christology*, Cambridge 1977.
104. Moule, op. cit., p. 101.
105. Ibid., p. 138.
106. Ibid., p. 139.
107. I believe that Colossians 1–3 was not written by Paul but by a disciple. I give my reasons in Chapter 4.
108. C. F. D. Moule, *The Birth of the New Testament*, London 1962, p. 67.
109. See *The Origin of Christology*, pp. 100–1.
110. V. Lossky, *The Mystical Theology of the Eastern Church*, third impression, London 1973, pp. 222–4.
111. Lossky, op. cit., pp. 231–2.

3. Paul and Pre-existence

1. J. D. G. Dunn, *Christology in the Making*, London 1980.
2. Dunn, op. cit., pp. 39f.
3. T. H. Colson and G. H. Whitaker trs., *Philo* in Loeb edition, London and Cambridge, Mass. 1934, vols V and VI.
4. Dunn, op. cit., p. 284, n. 153.
5. Ibid., pp. 40–1.
6. Ibid., p. 45.
7. Ibid., p. 50.
8. Ibid., p. 89.
9. Ibid., p. 107.
10. Ibid., p. 308, n. 41.
11. Ibid., pp. 108, 110, 111.
12. Ibid., p. 139.
13. See Philo, *De Opif. Mundi* 134 and *Leg. Alleg.* I, 31.
14. Dunn, op. cit., p. 124.
15. Ibid., pp. 119, 120, 120–1.
16. Ibid., p. 122.
17. Ibid., p. 151.
18. Ibid., p. 158.
19. Stuttgart 1966.
20. There is an alternative reading *tou theou* for *autou*, but it is very weakly attested. See C. K. Barrett, *The Gospel According to St John*, second edition, London 1978, in loc. Barrett accepts that John intends to refer to the pre-existent Christ here. See also P. Borgen, *Bread from Heaven*, London 1965, pp. 151, 175, for evidence that Christ is understood in the Fourth Gospel as having appeared in Israel's history.
21. Dunn. op. cit., p. 158.
22. Ibid., p. 56.
23. Ibid., pp. 288–9, n. 215.
24. H. G. Liddell and R. Scott (eds), *Greek-English Lexicon*, ninth edition, Oxford 1940.
25. The LXX translator has mistaken the Hebrew word ᶜāqēbh, which could mean 'footprint' hence 'succession', for ᶜēqebh, which means 'price, reward'.
26. It is true that Exod. 2.14 describes Moses as being afraid, but exegetical tradition would tend to put a good interpretation on Moses' action. It would be easy for some earlier exegete to read *wayiyra'* as *wayar'* 'and he saw'. Later legend elaborated the story of Moses' escape. See W. G. Braude, *The Midrash on the Psalms*, vol. 1, New Haven 1959, on Ps. 4.3, pp. 62–3. A series of legendary accounts of his escape is given, in which Moses is delivered from death at the hand of Pharaoh by miraculous intervention. The account in Hebrews had only reached the stage of assuming that Moses was not afraid. It is significant that Philo and Josephus in their respective accounts of the career of Moses make no mention of his being afraid of Pharoah.

(Philo, *De Vita Moses* I, 44–7; Josephus, *Antiquities* II, 254–7.) Philo represents him as a prospective candidate for the throne of Egypt; and Josephus, who does not even mention his killing of the Egyptian, has a piece of *haggada* about a successful war against the Ethiopians, which Moses waged on behalf of Egypt. It was this which caused the Egyptians in envy to plot his murder and thus necessitate his flight.

27. I expound this passage in my book *Jesus Christ in the Old Testament*, London 1965, pp. 72–5. Dunn summarily dismisses this work on p. 323, n. 115.

28. *Jesus Christ in the Old Testament*, pp. 65–72.

29. Dunn, op. cit., p. 55 and see p. 289, n. 218.

30. Ibid., pp. 183–4.

31. Ibid., p. 183.

32. Ibid., p. 330, n. 78.

33. Whether he ever uses allegory is another question which I have discussed in my *Studies in Paul's Technique and Theology*, London 1974, pp. 159–66.

34. Or 'the captivity of Israel'. The Hebrew is *sᵉbhi yiśrael*. See S. Schechter (ed.), *Documents of Jewish Sectaries Vol. I, Fragments of a Zadokite Work*, original edition Cambridge 1910, reissued Ktav Publishing USA, p. 113.

35. G. Vermes, *The Dead Sea Scrolls in English*, London 1962, p. 102.

36. G. G. Zunz, *The Text of the Epistles*, London 1953, pp. 126–7. See also p. 232. I owe this reference to my colleague Lionel North, Barmby Lecturer in the New Testament, and am most grateful for his drawing of my attention to it. In all honesty I should add that in the same work Zunz gives it as his opinion that *tupikōs* in verse 11 is not original, and that the original reading should be rendered: 'this happened to them; it was written for us' (pp. 233–4). If Zunz is right, it does not weaken my argument at all. If anything it throws doubt on Dunn's contention that Paul is giving us a consciously typological midrash. But I do not think it affects the argument very much either way.

37. Dunn, op. cit., p. 189.

38. Ibid., p. 190.

39. Ibid., p. 334, n. 121.

4. The Analogy of Pre-existence

1. The following pages are a paraphrase of a large part of an article, 'The Midrash in 2 Corinthians 3: A Reconsideration', which I published in the *Journal for the Study of the New Testament*, October 1980. I have omitted much of the technical detail.

2. *Tractate Yebamoth* 49.6 in the Babylonian Talmud, I. Epstein (ed.), London 1935. *Tractate Yebamoth* is edited by W. Slotki, 1936.

3. *Tractate Hagiga* ed., I. Abrahams, 1938.

4. J. Jervell, *Imago Dei*, Göttingen 1960, p. 117. The Rabbis actually borrowed the Greek word *eikōn* and transliterated it into Aramaic.

5. *Pesikta Rabbati*, ed. W. G. Braude, New Haven and London 1968,

Piska 33.11. The *Pesikta Rabbati* is a collection of homilies delivered by Rabbis on festal occasions, dating from the second or third centuries AD onwards.

6. See op. cit., London 1973, pp. 161–9, and J. D. G. Dunn, 'I Corinthians 15.45: Last Adam, Life-giving Spirit', in B. Lindars and S. Smalley (eds), *Christ and Spirit in the New Testament*, Cambridge 1973, pp. 127–41; and - *Unity and Diversity in the New Testament*, London 1977, pp. 84–91. See also his article 'II Corinthians 3.17: "The Lord is the Spirit"', in *Journal of Theological Studies*, new series, 21, 1970. I do deal with his argument there to some extent in my article 'The Midrash in 2 Corinthians 3'; see pp. 14, 16, 19, 20.

7. O. Cullmann, *The Christology of the New Testament*, ET London 1959, pp. 168–9, 181.

8. E. Eltester, *Eikon im Neuen Testament*, Tübingen 1958, p. 133; Jervell, op. cit., p. 180.

9. R. P. Martin, *Carmen Christi*, Cambridge 1967, p. 119.

10. R. G. Hamerton-Kelly, *Pre-existent Wisdom and the Son of Man*, Cambridge 1973, pp. 123., 152., 270f.

11. Martin, op. cit., p. 133.

12. Dunn, 'I Corinthians 15.45: Last Adam', p. 140.

13. Jervell, op. cit., pp. 259, 327; Martin, op. cit., p. 133. C. K. Barrett, *From First Adam to Last*, London 1962, pp. 75–6. The discussion of this point in the last chapter was orientated more towards Dunn's general position.

14. Cullmann, op. cit., p. 181; see also p. 169.

15. E. Larsson, *Christus als Vorbild*, Uppsala 1962, pp. 319–20.

16. Jervell, op. cit., p. 100.

17. I would draw this conclusion from a passage such as II Cor. 4.13, where as I interpret him, Paul represents Christ as actually uttering Psalm 116. But Psalm 116 is a psalm in which the devotee pleads for salvation from death.

18. This, I think, is implied in Paul's midrash on Deut. 30.12–14 in Rom. 10.6–7. We know from the Neofiti Targum that this passage in Deuteronomy was interpreted as referring to Moses' ascent to Sinai and Jonah's descent into the abyss. Paul sees these as types of the incarnation and *descensus ad inferos*. Compare also Phil. 2.10. It is in Philippians also that we find the nearest equivalent to the concept of 'a glorified humanity' in Paul. See Phil. 3.21, where Paul writes of Christ's 'glorious body' (*tō/i sōmati tēs doxēs autou*). But we do not have any contact with this glorious body till the Parousia; in the meantime Paul seems to envisage the possibility of a direct relationship to Christ after death; see the obscure passage II Cor. 5.6–10.

19. See my book *Jesus Christ in the Old Testament*, London 1965, Chapter 3, and see my argument in the previous chapter.

20. So I interpret Heb. 5.7–10. I do not regard the view that he was delivered from the fear of death as defensible.

21. See C. F. D. Moule, *The Origin of Christology*, Cambridge 1977, pp. 100f.
22. R. E. Brown, *The Community of the Beloved Disciple*, London 1979, p. 163.
23. And see *Jesus Christ in the Old Testament*, pp. 65–72.
24. As we noted on p. 79 above.
25. Colossians is another question in this respect. I have traced a very elaborate piece of typology in Col. 2.14–15, and typology is a step towards a doctrine of Christ's activity in Israel's history. See my *Studies in Paul's Technique and Theology*, London 1974, Chapter 1.
26. For reference in Philo see *De Conf. Ling.* 145–6; *De Somniis* 1.215; *De Plantatione* 9; *De Fug. et Invent.* 112; *De Mig. Abraham* 220; *Leg. Alleg.* III.96.
27. *De Vit. Mos.* II, 65 quoted by both J. B. Lightfoot, *The Epistles of St Paul: Colossians and Philemon*, London 1897, and C. F. D. Moule, *The Epistles to the Colossians and Philemon*, Cambridge 1958 in loc.
28. As a matter of fact I think it probable that the word 'Son' is not the original reading here. 'God only begotten' or even perhaps more likely 'the Only-begotten' was what John wrote.
29. I have expounded this in *The New Testament Interpretation of Scripture*, London 1980, pp. 110–14.
30. See my two articles 'John's citation of Psalm LXXXVI' in *New Testament Studies* 11, 1965, pp. 158–62, and 'John's citation of Psalm LXXXVI Reconsidered' in *New Testament Studies* 13, 1966, pp. 363–7.
31. This interpretation, or something like it, is supported by B. F. Westcott, *The Gospel According to St John*, London 1908, 2 vols; M.-J. Lagrange, *L'Évangile selon Saint Jean*, third edition, Paris 1947; R. Bultmann, *Das Evangelium des Johannes*, fifteenth impression, Göttingen 1962; E. Hoskyns and F. N. Davey, *The Fourth Gospel*, revised edition, London 1947; C. K. Barrett, *The Gospel According to St John*, London 1955; and J. N. Sanders and B. A. Mastin, *The Gospel According to St John*, London 1968.
32. W. G. Wilson, *The Faith of an Anglican*, London 1980.
33. Ignatius, *Ephesians* xix: *theou anthropinōs phaneroumenou*; see my comment in *The New Testament Interpretation of Scripture*, pp. 32f.

5. *Models and Objections*

1. Keith Ward, 'Incarnation or Inspiration – a False Dichotomy', *Theology*, July 1977, pp. 251–5.
2. See above p. 16.
3. G. W. H. Lampe, *God as Spirit*, Oxford 1977.
4. See above p. 42.
5. Martelet, *The Risen Christ and the Eucharistic World*, p. 136. See his sentence, already quoted on p. 48 above, where he uses the phrase 'identical and yet different' to describe the relationship.
6. R. H. Gundry, *Sōma in Biblical Theology*, Cambridge 1976.
7. In the two paragraphs that follow, I have made considerable use of the

section on the eucharist in a book which my brother and I have recently published: A. T. and R. P. C. Hanson, *Reasonable Belief*, Oxford 1981.

8. See *A Critique of Eucharistic Agreement*, London 1975.

9. Martelet, op. cit., p. 135.

10. Ibid., p. 113.

11. Ibid., pp. 115–16.

12. Ibid., p. 125.

13. Ibid., p. 161.

14. Ibid., p. 164.

15. Ibid., p. 178.

16. The 1662 revision did nothing to alter this strongly Anselmic emphasis.

17. Martelet, op. cit., p. 136.

18. Ibid., p. 151.

19. See J. Meyendorff, *Byzantine Theology*, London 1974, p. 203.

20. E.g. *Pesikta Rabbati*, Piska 5.11; cf. my *The New Testament Interpretation of Scripture*, p. 108.

21. Or 'an author of the Book of Wisdom' for it is possible that the authorship changes at the early part of Chapter 12.

22. P. Schoonenberg, *Covenant and Creation*, ET London 1968, 2, 14.

23. J. Moltmann, *The Crucified God*, pp. 188–9.

24. I have explained why I think this, and not 'reflecting', is the correct rendering; see my article 'The Midrash in 2 Corinthians 3, a Reconsideration' (Ch. 4 n. 1 above), pp. 21–2.

25. M. Hengel, *The Son of God*, ET London 1976.

26. G. W. H. Lampe, 'The Holy Spirit and the Person of Christ', in S. W. Sykes and J. P. Clayton (eds), *Christ, Faith and History*, Cambridge 1972, pp. 111–30. See pp. 120, 122, 129–30.

27. Lampe, *God as Spirit*, pp. 2, 3.

28. Ibid., p. 18.

29. Ibid., p. 33.

30. Ibid., p. 118.

31. Ibid., pp. 117–18.

32. Ibid., p. 41.

33. Ibid., p. 72.

34. Ibid., p. 103.

35. Ibid., p. 106.

36. Ibid., pp. 135–6.

37. Ibid., p. 136.

38. I have amalgamated Barth's 'mode of existence' with Rahner's 'manner of subsistence'. I believe they mean the same thing.

39. Lampe, op. cit., p. 140.

6. The Anthropomorphic God

1. H. W. Wolff, *Hosea*, ET Philadelphia 1974; J. L. Mays, *Hosea*, London 1969.

2. Quoted in W. R. Harper, *A Critical and Exegetical Commentary on Amos and Hosea*, Edinburgh 1905.

3. W. Rudolph, *Hosea*, Gütersloh 1965.

4. A. Weiser, *Das Buch der zwölf kleinen Propheten*, Göttingen 1963.

5. R. C. Moberly, *Atonement and Personality*, London 1901.

6. K. Elliger, *Deuterojesaja Vol 1*, Neukirchen-Vluyn 1973.

7. G. A. F. Knight, *Deutero-Isaiah*, New York 1965.

8. Knight, op. cit., in loc.

9. P.-E. Bonnard, *Le Second Isaie*, Paris 1972, my translation.

10. C. Westermann, *Isaiah 40–66*, ET London 1969.

11. R. N. Whybray, *Isaiah 40–66*, London 1975.

12. J. F. Stenning, *The Targum of Isaiah*, Oxford 1949.

13. Piska 29/30, 1, Vol. 2, 568. Compare K. G. Kuhn (ed.), *Sifre zu Numeri*, Stuttgart 1959, pp. 227, 688.

14. Bonnard, op. cit., in loc.

15. See Chapter 5 note 21, p. 176 above about the authorship of Wisdom.

16. See Chapter 4, p. 88 above.

17. See my *Studies in the Pastoral Epistles*, London 1968, Chapter 5. I do not, of course, hold that Paul wrote the Pastorals.

18. See M. F. Wiles, *The Spiritual Gospel*, Cambridge 1960, p. 137.

19. Moltmann, *The Crucified God*, p. 27. Moltmann appositley quotes Aristotle: 'it would be absurd if anyone were to assert that he loved Zeus' (p. 268). Compare also P. Schoonenberg, *Covenant and Creation*, p. 23. Israelite culture was 'a culture which was not yet capable of forming the purified concepts of our metaphysical theology'.

20. See my essay in *Studies in the Pastoral Epistles*, Chapter 4.

21. See above p. 126.

22. A. J. Heschel, *The Prophets*, New York and Evanston 1962.

23. Heschel, op. cit., p. 225.

24. Ibid., p. 226.

25. Ibid., p. 230.

26. Ibid.

27. Ibid., p. 231.

28. Ibid.

29. The verb is used in the LXX to translate the Hebrew verb *nasa'*, which can mean both 'take away' and 'bear'; and the reference seems to be to Isaiah 53.4, 12.

7. *The Heavenly Intercession*

1. See my article 'The Midrash in II Corinthians 3; a Reconsideration'.

2. See my *The New Testament Interpretation of Scripture*, pp. 69–70.

3. See Col. 1.8; 1.9; 3.16. The two last use the adjective *pneumatikos*. In 2.5 *en pneumati* does not refer to the Holy Spirit.

4. I take Ephesians to have been written by one who was a member of

the Pauline school, but who wrote at some distance in time from Paul. There are links with I Peter and the Pastoral Epistles. See my *Studies in the Pastoral Epistles*, Chapter 7.

5. F. F. Bruce, *Commentary on the Epistle to the Hebrews*, Edinburgh 1964.

6. C. Spicq, *L'Épitre aux Hébreux*, Paris 1952, vol. 2.

7. H. Strathmann, *Der Brief an die Hebräer* in *Das NT Deutsch*, Göttingen 1963.

8. See H. Windisch, *Der Hebräerbrief*, Tübingen 1913; the reference can be found in R. H. Charles, *Apocrypha and Pseudepigrapha of the Old Testament*, Oxford 1913, p. 811. It occurs according to his division at 7.12 of the Damascus Document. 'They also polluted their holy spirit.' In modern notation CD 5.12.

9. H. Montefiore, *The Epistle to the Hebrews*, London 1964.

10. E. C. Wickham, *The Epistle to the Hebrews*, London 1910.

11. O. Kuss, *Der Brief an die Hebräer*, Regensburg 1966.

12. B. F. Westcott, *The Epistle to the Hebrews*, second edition, London 1892.

13. Windisch, in loc., 9.14.

14. J. Hering, *L'Épitre aux Hébreux*, Neuchâtel and Paris 1954.

15. J. Moffatt, *A Critical and Exegetical Commentary on the Epistle to the Hebrews*, Edinburgh 1924. W. Manson, *The Epistle to the Hebrews*, London 1951. I say 'apparently', because Moffatt clothes his explanation in such a cloud of idealistic language that it is not easy to see what exactly he means. Manson follows suit.

16. See my *New Testament Interpretation of Scripture*, pp. 128–9.

17. I have expounded this interpretation of Paul more fully in *Jesus Christ in the Old Testament*, pp. 147–52 à propos II. Cor. 5.16–62.

18. See R. E. Brown, *The Community of the Beloved Disciple*, London 1979, pp. 109f.

19. See my *Studies in the Pastoral Epistles*, Chapter 5. See also my reference to this passage in Job on p. 40 above.

20. Philo, *Quis Rev. Div. Heres*, XLII, 20f.

21. J. K. Mozley, *The Doctrine of the Atonement*, London 1915, p. 206.

22. Ibid., p. 221.

23. See S. Benko, *Protestanten, Katholiken, und Maria*, Hamburg 1972, p. 46.

24. V. Lossky, *The Mystical Theology of the Eastern Church*, London 1957, p. 194.

25. Quoted by Tait, *The Heavenly Session of Our Lord*, p. 118.

26. See J. G. Davies, *He Ascended into Heaven*, p. 121; this sentence has already been quoted on p. 26 above. Contrast Schillebeeckx, *Christ*, p. 482, where he repudiates the idea that a true doctrine of the atonement requires 'the diminution of the wrath of God through some soothing action'.

27. Karl Barth, *Church Dogmatics*, II, 1, pp. 152, 396.

28. O. C. Quick, *Essays in Orthodoxy*, London 1916, pp. 97–8.

29. Lossky, op. cit., pp. 194–5.

30. Benko, op. cit., p. 47.

31. Ibid., p. 49. He is quoting the two encyclicals *Ubi Primum* (1849) and *Ineffabilis Deus* (1854).

32. P. Evdomikov, *L'Orthodoxie*, Neuchâtel and Paris 1968, pp. 148, 153–4.

33. See above p. 35.

INDEX OF SCRIPTURE REFERENCES